A
Biblical Perspective
on
ALCOHOLISM

by

Darryl R. Sletten

TO SOW IS TO HARVEST

Scythe Publications, Inc.

A Division of Winston-Derek Publishers Group, Inc.

First printing

PUBLISHED BY SCYTHE PUBLICATIONS, INC.
Nashville, Tennessee 37205

Library of Congress Catalog Card No: 93-61291
ISBN: 1-55523-658-8

Printed in the United States of America

I would like to thank my former pastor and friend, Reverend Rudolph Maurer of Lewiston, Minnesota for his wise counsel and help with this book and also my wife, Myrna, for her assistance in editing, typing and other factors necessary to get this book into print.

Most of all, I thank my Lord and Savior Jesus Christ for making this book possible.

Contents

Introduction

As a gratefully recovered alcoholic, I wish to give some helpful insights into the true nature of alcoholism and how to attain lifelong sobriety. Chronic drunkenness or abusive drinking are more appropriate terms to use.

Some are personally affected by this habit while others are aware of a relative, friend, acquaintance or family member who is an abusive drinker. My purpose in writing this book is to give scriptural guidance on alcohol habituation and to give future, current and already recovered abusive drinkers a responsible perspective on excessive drinking. Many Christians realize what the true nature of alcoholism is but are at a loss to explain it to the satisfaction of others, due to the confusing and varied theories expounded by those in the medical and psychological professions. It is often the tendency in today's society for people to believe whatever they don't understand. This is especially true when a theory or concept comes from highly educated and respected people working in the fields of science, medicine, and human behavior. This book will attempt to make it possible to understand that Scripture is clear concerning the real nature of alcoholism.

Included is a brief history about the use of wine in Biblical times and some theories on the causes of abusive drinking. A complete and thorough technical discussion of the various disease theories isn't necessary because Holy Scripture has the correct and definitive answers to the causes of abusive drinking. The more important medical theories about abusive drinking will be presented. Many theories are in circulation today about alcoholism and confusion would result if all the theories were presented here.

Lastly, I will try to show what help is available to abusers of alcohol and what kind of help is really needed in the counseling area for persons with problems of life. These problems include more than just alcohol abuse and can result in many other destructive habits. As history and our past transgressions should teach us, I hope my experiences will help others avoid unnecessary confusion and bring them to the source of true understanding and the help of the One we all need. The treatment theories and processes for alcoholism have been copied by other problem of life therapies. This is important in showing that the true perspective on alcoholism is applicable to the treatment of other habits.

In the following chapters I will show there is hope for abusers of alcohol and for others who are practicing harmful habits.

1

BIBLICAL HISTORY OF ALCOHOL USAGE

A good place to begin is with a brief history of the use and abuse of wine in Biblical times. Wine was a very common drink in Biblical days, as coffee is today. Dysentery of several types was endemic, and drinking water was easily contaminated. Wine was therefore a safe beverage because of its alcoholic content. Holy Scripture speaks of wine in several places. When Isaac gave Jacob his blessing, he said, "May God give you an abundance of grain and new wine" (Genesis 27:28). There is also the well-known record of Jesus miraculously changing water into wine. It is true that some Hebrews drank wine to excess. The Bible warns frequently and emphatically against excessive drinking.

There are many evidences in Scripture that alcoholic intoxication was one of the major social evils of ancient times. This was true of all nations, including Israel, the Near East and the Mediterranean world. Drunkenness was common among all classes, especially the rich and nobility (I Samuel 25:36; II Samuel 13:28; I Kings 16:9; 20:16). The Prophet Amos said that God would bring judgment upon the wealthy women of Samaria for enticing their husbands to drink with them. The fact that Eli suspected Hannah, the mother of Samuel, of being inebriated while she was engaged in prayer in the Tabernacle shows that intoxication was not unknown even in that holy place. Isaiah wrote about priests and prophets who reeled and staggered with strong drink and whose minds were confused with wine (Isaiah 28:7).

The Old Testament vividly describes the effects of strong drink. There are frequent references to the excessive consumption of wine and its effects on a person. Among those mentioned are an unsteady gait, staggering and vomiting, quarrelsomeness, brawling, drinking early in the morning and continuing until late at night. Excessive drinking led to mental confusion and the disillusion that duties could be neglected, which resulted in the ending of their days in poverty, woe and sorrow.

Among the best known cases of drunkenness in the Old Testament are Noah, Lot, Habal, Uriah, Amnon; Elah, King of Israel; Ben-hadad, King of Syria; and thirty-two allied kings. Priests were forbidden to drink wine and other strong drink while on duty in the sanctuary. Nazarites were expected to abstain from intoxicating beverages during the period of their vows.

The Scriptures contain firm injunctions against strong drink. Drunkenness is also used in a metaphorical sense. A drunkard could be stoned to death to rid society of this evilness.

This brief history shows that the responsible drinking of wine was not condemned. Excessive and abusive use of wine leads to drunkenness, which is condemned. We must remember not to condemn the drinker but the act of drunkenness itself.

In modern times, many view alcoholism as a disease and treat it as such. The Bible treats it as a moral problem.

2

THEORIES ON ALCOHOLISM

It has become commonplace and generally acceptable to refer to alcoholism as a disease. Professionals in the fields of physical medicine, psychology, genetics, and pharmacology have studied alcoholism thoroughly, but remain puzzled. There are many theories which suggest causes, prevention, and treatment disciplines, but to date, there are no definitive answers from the medical profession. The one obvious fact is that if we do not ever drink alcohol we cannot ever become "addicted" to it.

What is alcoholism? The dictionary defines alcoholism as a chronic disorder characterized by dependence on alcohol, repeated and excessive consumption of alcoholic beverages, the development of withdrawal symptoms upon reducing or ceasing intake, morbidity that may include cirrhosis of the liver, and decreased ability to function socially and vocationally. A term used in relation to alcoholism is addiction. Addiction is described as a psychological and emotional dependence on a drug resulting from repeated usage but without the physiological need to increase dosage. Addiction is also described as a compulsive, uncontrollable dependence on a substance, habit or practice to the degree that cessation causes severe emotional, mental or physiological reactions. The term "uncontrollable" in this definition is disputable, and will be addressed later.

According to the dictionary, addiction is the state of being given to a practice or to something that is habit-forming, such as narcotics, to the extent that stopping use causes severe trauma. A habit is defined as a compulsive need, inclination, or use. Addiction is described as an acquired behavior pattern regularly followed until it becomes almost involuntary. "Almost" is a significant word and enforces the fact that addictive behavior is not completely involuntary as the term addiction infers.

A distinction must be made between the terms addiction and habituation. I believe a true habit or habituation refers to a person becoming conditioned through repeated usage or practice to continue a behavior that seems to offer them some sort of benefit. Habit, habitual, or habituation are appropriate terms to describe the abusive drinker's perceived need for the effects of alcohol. The dictionary defines habituation as accustoming a person to something. An example would be that wealth habituates someone to luxury.

If most people thought of addiction as having a meaning that does not involve a physical aspect to it, I would use that term. Since medical researchers consider physical addiction to be involved in alcohol abuse, I will use the term "habit" instead.

The medical establishment has also defined habituation as negative adaptation. It is ironic that their simple definition of addiction is that it is a lifestyle—a behavioral disorder. (I agree with this definition.) They state that alcohol abuse is a learned behavior cultivated by a habitual readiness to drink whenever a hurtful situation arises. They also refer to so-called addictions to many things and persons in addition to alcohol. Addiction is described not as a chemical reaction, but as an experience which grows out of a routine, subjective response to something that has special meaning for an individual. It is anything that he or she finds so safe and reassuring that they feel they cannot be without it.

4

Bad habits can come about from not being focused: with no compelling interest, philosophy, or clear purpose in life. Negative feelings contribute toward looking for the self-perceived emotional security of abusive drinking. Whenever the desire for emotional security takes priority over all else, habituation sets in. When life is seen as a burden, habituation is a way to surrender. A fearful person will seek support from an external force, such as alcohol, when faced with demands and problems.

The chief reason the medical establishment calls alcoholism an illness is the claim that the alcoholic cannot regain control if, after years of abstinence, the compulsion supposedly sets in again. The idea of lost control certainly is in dispute. They go on to sub-classify alcoholics into divisions, categories, classes, etc.

There are many theories which have been advanced on what causes alcoholism and what alcoholism is. Cultural, socioeconomic, hereditary, metabolic, psychological, pharmacological, nutritional, biochemical, brain pathology, allergies, and endocrinology are all factors taken into consideration. One interesting facet is that the term addiction is ordinarily used in a psychological or mental sense. This reminds us that humans are vulnerable to deception and are deluded in our thinking processes, as the situation of Eve and the serpent in the Garden of Eden reveals.

The number of theories offered in the alcoholism controversy is staggering. I personally counted thirty-three opinions or formulations in the branches of medicine alone. There are also various subgroups of theories within some of the formulations.

Though I disagree with many assumptions and conclusions professed by those in the field of psychology, there is wisdom in some of their formulations on alcoholism. They state that the drinking response becomes learned because it leads to a reduction in tension.

They also believe that frustrations, feelings of guilt and inferiority, resentments, and tensions are used to justify the postulation of a dependence on alcohol at a symbolic, or psychological level. They state that repetition enhances the desire to drink until it becomes a compulsion. Compulsion is not the correct word to use however, because it implies irresistible or, in a real sense, uncontrollable. The Biblical view of behaviors and the compulsion concept will be discussed in a later chapter.

Other ideas include the thinking that so-called addiction is habituation or constant repetition. It has been proposed that the anxiety reducing effects of alcohol may, if anxiety is great enough, constitute greater reinforcement than the competing punishment.

A newspaper article about an unorthodox chemical dependency treatment center said that at the facility chemical dependency and other disorders are seen as symptoms of a larger problem. In a similar context, new research suggests that depression might be the cause, not the result, of some drug abuse. It is further stated that these results fly in the face of conventional wisdom. This research estimates that ten to twenty percent of alcohol abusers fit this pattern. The percentage estimate is open to question but does illustrate that some researchers are beginning to look in a different direction for answers, as are some abusers. A former prostitute and drug abuser testified to a minister that she had found that drug abuse was a spiritual problem for her and felt that social programs just didn't address the issue from that standpoint.

The craving for alcohol or the effect of alcohol is referred to in both the physical and the psychological sense by the medical establishment. Physical craving occurs when someone drinks excessive alcohol for long periods of time and is supposedly manifested by symptoms upon withdrawal. They say psychological craving accounts for initial abuse. The craving or desire is not directed specifically at alcohol but at a desire to become intoxicated, to experience the desired euphoria.

There is confusion in pharmacology circles about what classification alcohol falls into in the addictive drug category. Alcohol is placed somewhere between addiction producing and habit forming drugs. The confusion in categorizing is expected. Alcohol is a nervous system depressant.

One factor seldom mentioned is the environmental factor and the importance of the home and setting in which a person grows up. Influences resulting from the observation, words, and actions of a parent who is an abusive drinker have a profound effect on impressionable children and adolescents.

This chapter on the disease theory tries to show that the contention of a disease process involving alcoholism is not very convincing. Many of the medical and psychological theories concerning alcoholism and its supposed etiologies are not included. Many are confusing and cloud the issue further, only giving more faulty theories to ponder. Some of the more theoretically convincing concepts, especially the genetic and biochemical concepts, are covered in a later chapter.

3

THOUGHTS ON ALCOHOLISM FROM EARLIER CENTURIES

In the eighteenth and nineteenth centuries, various people spoke out on drunkenness and gave their views as to its cause. The organized Temperance Society stated that "alcoholism which involves (surely at its inception as well as during development and possibly after its development) a decision as to whether to drink or not." The Women's Christian Temperance Union said the disease concept was restricted only to compulsive excessive drinkers. This statement shows confusion in the WCTU. Not until well past 1900 did WCTU literature begin to admit that later and sounder research had shown that alcohol use was not inheritable.

In 1784, Dr. Benjamin Rush issued a paper in which he deplored the despiritualizing effects of rum, making its victim "abandoned" to the last degree regardless of their duty to God. Abraham Lincoln, in 1842, said, "I believe if we take habitual drunkards as a class, their heads and their hearts will bear advantageous comparison with those of any other class. There seems ever to have been a proneness in the brilliant and the warm-blooded, to fall into this vice. The demon of intemperance ever seems to have delighted in sucking the blood of genius and generosity."

A Reverend Danforth, in 1830, believed that drunkenness keeps a person in a state of hardness of heart and blindness of mind. At Harvard Medical School, a Dr. Davis saw the typical drunkard as a maimed or unstable personality and said that nineteen in twenty alleged heredity cases he had seen obviously acquired the habit from home influences (environment) and not from heredity. (It is difficult to believe that even one case was considered hereditary.) Dr. Bucknill, of the New York Christian Home for Intemperate Men, mentioned the fallacy of the notion of inherited drunkenness. He observed that only twenty-eight of the one hundred and seventy-six drunks he worked with had parents who were also drunks. He stated that there is no gain in the establishment of a theory that drunkenness is a disease.

A paper written by Mr. J. E. Todd in 1882, stated emphatically that drunkenness is not a disease. A large portion of doctors agreed with him at that time. He said there is no such thing as a disease of the mind and that disease is always an affliction of the body. Drunkenness was said to be a vice or a habit of the nervous center, which energizes an emotional direction contrary to the well-being of the individual and the community. (We now realize that there is physical damage from long term abusive drinking.) Todd believed that by continuance and repetition, vices become inveterate and that vice is cured by removing the cause. He said the causes of disease were physical and the causes of vice were always moral. He went on to say that the drunkard is not subject to an irresistible propensity to drink and that he never met an instance of pure dipsomania. Another difference between drunkenness being a habit vs. a disease which he wrote about was that drunks were ashamed and remorseful after a bout of heavy drinking while a person with a disease isn't subject to either of these feelings.

There are various opinions amongst religious people about what to make of alcoholism. They agree that initial drunkenness is a sin, but as a person gets into repetitive, chronic, or heavy drinking, and long term drunkenness, questions arise concerning-whether or not the abuser is responsible for their behavior. This questioning is probably due to the strong influence of the medical establishment.

I feel that Holy Scripture has the answer to the true nature of alcoholism or chronic drunkenness.

4

DEFINITION OF DISEASE

The disease theory of alcoholism is readily accepted today. If we accept the encyclopedic definition of disease: "at its simplest level, disease can be defined as any deviation from normal form and function," then all deviations from normal patterns of mental and physical wellness can be considered disease.

There is an overwhelming misunderstanding of what the terms disease, illness, and health refer to. Many laypeople and medical personnel use the term "disease" incorrectly as they do not realize that the all encompassing definition is any deviation from man developed patterns in all areas of human behavior. Within this definition, any departure from a state of health is considered a disease, whether we measure health in theoretical terms of normal measured values or in more pragmatic terms of ability to function effectively in harmony with one's environment.

A questionnaire sent to more than two hundred Christian denominations brought back varying replies to the question, "How do you view alcoholism, in terms of sin, disease, or both?" Some wrote that their denominational view was that alcoholism was both a sin and a disease. Is this possible? The fields of secular physical medicine and psychology create confusion among Christian leaders.

Health is not a static condition, but represents a fluid range of physical and emotional well-being continually subjected to internal and external challenges such as worry, workloads, varying external temperatures, bacteria, and viruses. Health is defined in terms of certain measured values like body temperature, pulse rate, breathing rates, blood pressure, etc. Health should be thought of as not merely the absence of disease and illness, but also the ability to function in harmony with one's environment. An injury such as a broken ankle is considered a disease. If a person breaks his or her own ankle deliberately it is then considered a disease in two ways: mentally and physically.

Illness implies discomfort or inability to function optimally. It is possible to have a disease for many years without being aware of it. A person can be diseased, but not feel ill. An angry and frustrated person is not functioning effectively and in complete harmony with the environment. They could be considered to have a disease because their feelings would be considered a departure from the state of optimum health. This illustrates how broad the disease definition is that any deviation, be it mental, physical, or emotional, is considered abnormal and hence a disease. No wonder then that alcoholism, sexual addition, anorexia nervosa, bulimia, and other problems of life are considered a part of the category of disease.

Disease should be considered to be a physiological condition: that is, affecting the organs, tissues, glands, and various systems of the body directly. Disease is not the causative factor in the case of alcoholism, but the aftereffects or damage done to the body due to the toxic effects of the alcohol over time. The exception is alcohol overdose which can result in instant death. Many abusive drinkers have a poor diet. The lack of adequate nutrition can damage the body.

If we hold to the strict definition of the word, even stress or criminal behaviors could be considered diseases because they are not in harmony with one's environment.

If there is the slightest possibility of a physically addictive concept in alcoholism, it lies in the ability or trick of Satan to produce an insignificant physically addictive aspect, and in this way deceive people into believing alcoholism is a disease.

Many have overcome drunkenness. Further, if physical addiction did exist in alcoholism, it still would not be a disease in the true sense of what most people understand a disease to be! Even if insignificant physical manifestations are present that make it somewhat difficult to stop drinking, these problems may be hurdles God expects an abuser to suffer and overcome as the consequences of disobeying Him. To repeat, alcoholism is not a true disease no matter what you have heard or read. We must separate this act of immorality from the aftereffects caused by it.

A person willingly decides to drink. If alcoholism is a disease, it would have to be described as a disease one decides to get. Each person decides whether to drink or not, how much, and how often. Although a person may feel they have lost control over a long period of heavy drinking (as with other habits), they have not. Our minds may try to convince us that we cannot quit. Because we perceive that something isn't possible does not mean it actually is impossible, only extremely difficult, as in the case of chronic drunkenness. We can quit. Alcoholism is avoidable and in no way can be compared to, for instance, the disease of juvenile diabetes.

Alcoholism is a learned attitude and behavior and, in this respect, environmental processes are a factor. Rather than alcoholism, continued or habitual drunkenness or abusive drinking are the most truthful and descriptive terms to use. It is possible to quit abusive drinking but no one has been known to quit a disease, like diabetes.

An individual is personally responsible for beginning abusive drinking and for ending it. Today's pop psychology affirms the idea that things are not our fault. This trend teaches people to shift responsibility for their problems in life and bad habits to someone else: usually their parents. Everyone is affected by their home environment while growing up. This does not excuse us from repeating the same mistakes our parents made. Many who

15

come out of a difficult home life have learned not to repeat their parent's mistakes, attitudes, or behaviors. A bad example can teach a child to search for a better attitude or behavior and consequences of a parent's behavior can teach a valuable lesson.

Other people can help someone decide to stop abusive drinking, as do tragic consequences, but in the end, we are individually responsible for our decisions and actions.

The definition of disease is a major key in the disease versus sin dispute. What the average person perceives about what the term disease actually encompasses is very important. The popular definition of disease is: any deviation from the state of a normal pattern of mental and physical wellness. This definition should be limited to physiological references to avoid confusing the issue.

5

THE SINFUL NATURE AND ALCOHOLISM

We understand from Holy Scripture that all sin, disease, and death are a result of the fall of Adam and Eve. In John 9:1-3, Jesus was asked if it was the sin of the blind man or of his parents that was responsible for the blindness. Jesus said, "neither." He then went on to say, "it is no sin, either of this man or of his parents." The Book of Job clearly shows that Job's diseases were not the result of personal sin.

There are real and authentic diseases not caused from personal sin or a rejection of God. They may be allowed in order to let God's works show forth. There is a distinction between willful personal sins that can lead to disease (cirrhosis of the liver, venereal disease, AIDS, etc.) and being born with or later contracting a disease such as diabetes or cancer.

When Adam and Eve disobeyed God in the Garden of Eden, all future mankind was affected. All are born with a sinful nature and will individually disobey God. As Scripture testifies, the original sin of Adam and Eve led to the afflictions of disease, sickness, and death—events that happen to all persons. Without the original sin, there would be no disease.

Sickness, disease, and death are the result of man's inherited depravity or sinful nature. Individual sins vary from person to person. If this was not so, all of mankind would suffer exactly the same illnesses and diseases. Yet, sickness is not always a direct result of sin. Jesus' response in John 9:3 reflects the condition of man's sinfulness rather than a willful, specific act. This is so because when God created man, man was made perfect. Since the fall, God does allow disease. Disease can occur even in a person who is blameless in the sense that personal, specific sin was not responsible for his or her disease.

Willful, individual sin can be the direct cause of a disease. The general sinful condition of all mankind allows for disease to happen because of the original sin of Adam and Eve. The distinction between willful individual sin and the general sinful condition of all mankind is important.

An actual specific act of sin cannot at the same time be a disease. In what is called alcoholism (chronic drunkenness) the acts in themselves cannot be both sin and disease. This truth is ignored by modern thinking. God does not allow individual personal sin and disease to be the same. Since true diseases like leukemia, epilepsy, some cancers, and diabetes are thought of as unavoidable, then alcoholism, if considered a disease, would be thought of as unavoidable and outside of personal responsibility for an offense against God!

Alcoholism or chronic drunkenness is definitely avoidable. The act of drunkenness is an offense against God that can lead to or result in a true disease. Damaging physiological aftereffects of alcohol on body tissues and organs include cirrhosis of the liver.

The original act of drunkenness and repeated acts are an offense against God. Repetitive acts of alcohol abuse cannot be explained away as unavoidable and uncontrollable results of disease.

6

Hope for Alcoholics

Proper understanding of the term powerlessness is crucial when referring to the process of abusive drinking. We are all powerless to keep from offending God because of our sinful nature. Our sinful nature allows us to enter into alcoholism or chronic drunkenness. In the alcohol habituation cycle, an almost formidable degree of powerlessness appears when it becomes extremely difficult to control the urge for the effects that alcohol produces.

The first Step in the Alcoholics Anonymous manual reads: *We admitted we were powerless over alcohol—that our lives had become unmanageable.* Those in AA believe powerlessness is the recognition that a person has lost control over some aspect of his or her life. They also say: *"Ironically, one starts to gain personal power the very instant powerlessness is acknowledged. With this acknowledgement comes the realization that a person has control over and can only change one thing—SELF."*

These statements are confusing, misleading, contradictory, and untrue. The words, "powerlessness," "lost control" and "ironically," must be looked at carefully. Powerlessness means being unable to exercise any power in a situation. Lost control means the same. As used here, the term ironically means out of the ordinary or normally not expected to happen.

It is difficult to understand how AA can use a term like powerlessness and contradict themselves by saying it is possible not to be powerless. Since many alcoholics have stopped their destructive habit, then the term powerlessness does not apply at all. There *is* power. There is the power of the affected individual who may quit for external reasons not relating to God, and especially the power of Christ to help us lead the life He desires for us.

Understanding about habituation in general and our freedom of choice specifically is essential to deal with the often fatal, both in an earthly and spiritual sense, process called alcoholism. We can reject Christ of our own choice. It is the Holy Spirit alone who brings us to faith in Christ. It is nothing we do through our own strength or will. Being a Christian does not exempt a person from making bad choices or acting against the will of God. We are constantly subject to the conflict between the flesh and the spirit until the day we die. In the overall picture of life, God is responsible for everything but sin. The Christian recognizes this and God's power and strength to help us. Psalm 73:21-26 says, "my flesh and my heart fail, but as long as I can cry in the midst of my crassest sins, nevertheless I am continually with Thee." Those who do not believe should reconsider their rejection of God in light of His promises. It may seem wonderful for the unbeliever to stop chronic drunkenness, yet it is not a good work in God's sight (Isaiah 64:6).

Through the grace and power of God we have been given freedom to choose between the flesh and the Spirit. A Christian who chooses to begin abusive drinking can also choose to stop this offense against God. Sometimes believers, like unbelievers, will stop their habit for reasons not relating to God. An individuals' motivation for desiring to stop a sinful habit is of the utmost importance to God. God's miracle of help for the chronic drinker occurs when the repentant believer asks Him for help by placing faith and trust in Him. Then Christ will create within the person the desire and ability to obey Him and to do that which is His will. When one is in Christ, their desire is to please Him above all and to glorify God in all they do. This is the real miracle. It is not that God somehow waves a magic wand and we stop abusive drinking. God looks at the heart of a believer and desires that we repent daily for transgressions against Him.

Although the unbeliever and unrepentant believer may stop chronic abusive drinking for external reasons not relating to God, they are missing God's promises to them. It is not that we cannot stop abusive drinking on our own, but the real issue to God is the motivation to stop our sinful habit: to please ourselves and man or to please God is the ultimate issue.

Verses two and three of the fourth chapter of the book of James read, "You do not obtain because you do not ask. You ask and you do not receive because you ask wrongly, with a view to squandering what you receive on your pleasures." What we ask must be according to God's will. This verse could apply to believers who ask God and receive not. They should look at where they are in their faith.

God is responsible for everything that is not of sin, and is involved in everyone's life. He allows us to reject him and commit individual sins if we so choose. In this sense, we can look at drunkenness and quitting the sinful habit from a different perspective.

Alcohol habituation is only one of many harmful and often destructive habits. Human beings are prone to forming habits. We become habituated to less harmful practices than alcohol. We develop habits and repetitive patterns in our daily lives. Many are necessary and good, like going to work on time, brushing our teeth, obeying traffic signs, and going to church. When a habit or any other thing becomes more important to us than God, it is then a sinful habit. Things and people must never be more important to us than God is.

The obvious common sense meaning of the term obsessive compulsive behavior describes habituation well. One author stated that drug researchers Chein, Winick and Zinberg have convincingly shown that it is not drugs that cause addiction, but people who addict themselves.

In His wisdom, God works in mysterious ways to help us avoid the human inclination of trying to earn our way into heaven by doing good works. Some Scripture that is difficult to understand allows for differences of opinion so we do not become robot-like followers. This curtails our natural inclination to obey in a legalistic way. This is only true in the occurrence of Bible verses that are difficult to understand and where there may be some degree of latitude in interpretation.

Harmful habituation can also include a materialistic object, amounting to idol worship. Anything that is uppermost in importance and always on our minds must be guarded against. We must not let anything become so important that it becomes more vital than our Creator. Worldly goods must be held in a proper perspective as should the importance of our families and people in general.

Compulsive behavior occurs when a person has such an extremely strong urge to do something that it appears he or she is under the binding control of the compulsion. Obsession is when something is constantly on ones mind and seems to drive a person to the point where they ignore many other areas of their life.

Compulsion is generally referred to as mental in scope, but physical medicine researchers appear to give a physiological aspect to so-called compulsion or compulsive behaviors. Although a medical dictionary does not refer to abusive drinking as a sign of compulsive behavior, the pattern of alcohol abuse could fit quite well into the definition. The definition explains compulsion as an irresistible, repetitive, irrational impulse to perform an act that is usually contrary to one's ordinary judgments or standards and which results in overt anxiety if not completed.

In the Formula of Concord, Epitome, Article II, Free Will, under "Contrary False Doctrine" it is stated: "Accordingly, we reject and condemn all the following errors as being contrary to the norm of the Word of God: (note: I refer only to the first error) 1. The mad dream of the so-called Stoic philosophers and of the Manichaeans who taught that whatever happens must so happen and could not happen otherwise, that man always acts under compulsion, even in his external acts, and that he commits evil deeds and acts like fornication, robbery, murder, theft, and similar sins under compulsion."

Since the compulsion concept is contrary to the norm of the Word of God, then the ideas and theories of medical researchers stating that alcohol abuse is an uncontrollable disease must also be rejected. The belief that a chronic abuser is compelled physiologically to continue abusive drinking is contrary to the Word of God and false. This would apply to other habitual behaviors that medical researchers may have theorized as physiological in nature as well. This error in the interpretation of compulsive behaviors is overlooked and neglected by many Christians and pastors who have felt societal pressure to follow theories of well-respected and highly educated medical researchers. Scientific education, while valuable in many areas, is sometimes in conflict with the Word of God.

Are all bad habits considered a disease by the mental health professions? The answer would have to be "yes" if you refer to the definition of disease. There are many misconceptions of the disease concept due to the fields of physical medicine and psychology reporting erroneous theories. As a result, most investigators feel that alcoholism, as a disease, is not curable. Rather than discuss all such theories, which would lead to more confusion, it is wiser to look at what appears to be the true position on how to view chronic drunkenness.

Anyone can become an alcohol abuser. The problem is not restricted to certain persons. We are all susceptible to forming habits. The genetic theory of possible inherent tendencies from birth to become a future alcoholic is not proven and is no doubt a fallacy. A study has shown that eighty-two percent of male children with an alcoholic parent do not become alcoholics. Most alcoholics have parents who were not alcoholic. Often in adolescents, the experience of habituation is more a matter of fixation than full blown habituation, though this does not minimize the seriousness of consuming excessive alcohol.

In my personal situation, there were underlying conflicts present. My fear of failure and not wanting to admit I could fail led to selfish and dishonest decisions. Instead of looking to God for help, I used lies to cover my weaknesses and inadequacies. I suffered so much mental and emotional stress in the actual decision making process, that often I made no decision at all. Conflicts between the moral and immoral burned inside me and often I made a selfish, immoral decision. The indecision and wrong decisions left me with much guilt. I looked for some way to cope with this stress and guilt. The coping resulted in alcohol abuse.

Proverbs 31:4-7 describes my situation at that time: "It is not for kings to drink wine, nor for princes intoxicating drinks; lest they drink and forget the law and pervert the justice of all the afflicted. Give strong drink to him who is perishing, and wine to those who are bitter of heart; let him drink and forget his poverty and remember his misery no more." One study of verse six of this proverb states: "It is supposed to have been in consideration of the injunction in the text that the ladies of Jerusalem provided the criminals, on their way to the place of execution, a drink of medicated wine, which might deaden the pain of suffering." Verse seven, according to the same writer, concerns itself with the rich giving wine to the poor when "thus is shown a way in which the rich can comfort and encourage their poorer brethren, which is a better method of using God's good gifts than by expending them on their own selfish enjoyment."

Another student of the Bible writes, "The Hebrew Sage also believed that wine was a source of joy and comfort for the despairing and dying." This writer also said, "strong drink evidently has its proper use according to the wise men, although they deprecate overindulgence."

Deep emotional hurts, severe feelings of inadequacy, and painful experiences often lead to habituation if not dealt with positively, including asking God for guidance. There are two primary reasons a person drinks. One is for enjoyment and relaxation, while the other is to cope with emotional turmoil such as guilt, pain, and feelings of hopelessness or inadequacy. If these conditions are not dealt with they can produce a diminishing and unhealthy effect on a person's sense of good conscience in a continuing pattern as time goes on. Some may become almost totally unfeeling persons. Such people attempt to block guilt by trying to erase it from their minds through alcoholic habituation. The unfeeling person tries to justify and accept guilt as an almost normal part of his or her mental makeup, instead of merely trying to block it out with alcohol. The person who tries to justify bad attitudes and behaviors, whether an abuser of alcohol or not, has a seriously diminished sense of good conscience.

Individuals with unresolved inner conflict look for a stress reliever and alcohol is a way to temporarily forget, as well as experience an euphoric effect and seemingly gain the ability to cope. The feelings and highs he or she gains from the initial heavy drinking appear as an ideal substitute for dealing with and coping soberly with conflicts and problems. One recovered alcohol abuser who is now a counselor operating a Christian counseling center, has said that he knows from personal and professional experience that the medical model of alcoholism removes the very factor that decreases recidivism: personal responsibility for how one deals with life. He has found that those who come to terms with the underlying causality that led them to become abusers tend not to return for additional inpatient stays in treatment centers.

A Christian writer has written, "Alcoholism is usually a form of escape from an unpleasant or intolerable situation. When life becomes unduly burdensome, when the individual is crushed by a sense of inferiority or frustration, when circumstances seem to place too heavy a load upon him, he looks for some way of escape. He hungers for temporary oblivion." He also writes, "For all practical purposes he has indulged in some self-anesthetization." He further says, "A change in drinking habits can hardly occur unless such a man has a change in his life philosophy."

Alcohol abuse also can lead a person to become involved in acts, which when sober, will cause remorse and guilt. Guilt increases and becomes a cycle while the effects of alcohol become so important that he or she will say or do almost anything to be under the influence.

Drunkenness brings out resentments not present in a sober state. This is due to the lack of inhibition caused by alcohol. Alcohol abusers may have problems relating to others, especially those with whom they have the closest personal relationships. Alcoholics are not only victims of their own abuse, but are the agents of its cause. Sinning against God and man becomes easier when under the influence. The mind becomes preoccupied with the next drink and other areas of life suffer. It is easy to become dishonest, conniving, selfish, and sometimes abusively aggressive in the continuing and deteriorating cycle of chronic drinking. An alcoholic may be forced to take some action at the point when people close to them have had enough of their abusive lifestyle and they are hitting bottom due to physical or job problems, accidents, financial troubles, etc. Of course there are abusive drinkers who stop the habit before it reaches a crisis situation.

An astute author questioned the commonly professed thinking of many so-called experts on alcoholism treatment concerning the "whys", or reasons, to quit alcohol abuse. She said, "you have been told, as have your loved ones, that unless you want to stop drinking for your sake, any attempts to get you to do so will fail. That concept is based on an untruth originated by the father of lies. No delusion is more cunningly contrived than that one. None is more devious."

She also said, "It's time you realized you should stop drinking for the sake of My people." (Note: This author was writing in the context of how she felt God may state this to an alcohol abuser.) She felt that an alcohol abuser should stop his or her abuse for the sake of others—spouse, children, parents and others who have to deal with the abuser. She makes a very good point.

In addition, she felt that the abuser should turn their sinful side to God and that God will draw the abuser unto Himself and give the power to live a new life. This is hope for all alcohol abusers and others caught up in sinful habits.

Family, friends, clergy and other concerned persons help motivate, encourage and support a loved one who abuses alcohol. Crisis intervention is sometimes done when these people confront the abuser and attempt to convince him or her of the destructiveness of alcohol abuse. This not only helps the abuser personally, but can help prevent further damage to the family and friends of the abuser in addition to saving innocent lives in highway accidents.

Some chronic drinkers refuse help even when the possibility of serious consequences arises. Some have suicidal thoughts and try to kill themselves. When an offense against civil law is committed, state courts may order treatment for an abuser who is in imminent danger of harming himself or others.

During the treatment process, (ideally done at a Christian treatment center) the main conflict or conflicts within the abuser's heart and mind are dealt with. If they are not, he or she may only temporarily stop drinking. To stop drinking is not enough. It is necessary to replace old behaviors with new and righteous behaviors. Stopping a habit does not transform a life. God's Word is needed to stay free and be the person He desires us to be.

In plain words, what is alcoholism? To me it is a repetition of drunkenness to the point where one perceives the need for the effects of alcohol as vital to their continued existence. It supposedly helps me to forget and lose myself. Another description is: habituation to the effects of alcohol happens when the urge for the effects is so great that only replacing that urge with something more important will halt the habit. An abuser often has delusionary thinking about what they feel is important in life. To overcome this situation, outside help is vital. The most ideal help comes from God working through help-oriented individuals.

I used the effects of alcohol as a way of coping and to help me temporarily forget my weaknesses, fears, and guilts in life. When something good happened, alcohol became a reward or part of a celebration. If it was not for underlying fear and guilt, I would not have been a chronic abuser of alcohol.

Abusive drinking is not a condition itself but a symptom of underlying conflicts. Resolve the conflict and alcoholism will disappear. Spiritual involvement with God is the lasting type of help needed. Non-Christians put their faith in a higher power concept other than God. This can be a person, object, or figment of their imagination. The important difference between faith in God and faith in other higher powers is that God can and will help us if we but ask Him. The non-Christian has only their belief system and human willpower to help them not drink again.

It is a positive first step when nonbelievers and unrepentant believers stop abusing alcohol, but a belief and faith in Christ is what is needed. It is my prayer that nonbelievers will receive Christ and unrepentant believers will amend their ways and follow Christ.

Bill Wilson, cofounder of Alcoholics Anonymous, once participated in small Oxford group meetings that emphasized prayer, mutual confession, the importance of making restitution when you have wronged someone, and the importance of personal witness. The Oxford Group's goal of knowing more of Jesus was too religious for Bill. He developed a fellowship of alcoholics dedicated to helping one another stay sober through a spiritual program that recognized no dogma, no absolutes, and was open to all. In the AA program, the alcoholic is asked to believe not in Jesus but in a higher power than ourselves.

Alcoholics Anonymous has helped abusers admit they have a drinking problem and has offered support to them. The organization has helped people stop the destructive habit and many of them have become involved in a church. This has been positive for families and communities.

Unfortunately, the pluralism of beliefs in the higher power concept, the unscriptural aspects of some psychological help, and the disease theory have done serious harm to Christians and potential Christians. To stop drinking alone is not enough. More is needed to live our lives as God desires. Holy Scripture should be our guide for life—not philosophy that contradicts Scripture.

In chemical dependency treatment centers today, the emphasis is on psychology. These centers have fewer long term successes than thought. They expound anti-Christian ideas that come from secular psychology. There is a real need for Christian groups and treatment centers for alcohol abusers, and qualified Christian counselors. Biblical help is important from the beginning. Church pastors should not delegate counseling to non-Christian sources. Troubled Christians with problems of life need knowledgeable Christian counselors. Fellow Christians who have experienced similar problems can be peer counselors.

The church has relinquished much of the counseling of troubled Christians to secular psychologists. One Christian leader said that the field of psychology interferes wrongly in the Christian area of problems of life. He felt that those in the field of psychology should concentrate on true mental conditions. Perhaps he meant retardation, brain injuries, brain diseases, and diseases that affect the brain, although in reality these are medical conditions. Secular psychology sometimes ventures into the realm of religion in its counseling presuppositions and methods. A counselor should use scriptural terminology for sinful patterns that dominate people's lives, rather than psychological terms.

The trend that AA began in its group therapy sessions and twelve steps for recovering from alcoholism is now copied by other "isms" that in reality, are problems of life. The Veteran's Administration denied educational benefits to veterans who were alcoholics and did not use their benefits within the prescribed time allowed. The VA called alcoholism "a case of willful misconduct." It is confusing to be told that alcoholism is considered a disease, yet see abusive drinkers penalized for transgressions of the law. What disease that is a legitimate physical affliction is legally penalized?

The field of psychology complicates moral issues and confuses laypeople with its explanations, definitions, and terminology. Psychologists declare themselves experts but in reality, no one can truly understand the human mind or predict what a person will think. One psychologist candidly said that a coin toss is as accurate as the psychologists opinion in determining whether a released prison inmate will go back to crime or not.

7

A Look at Scripture

If God considered chronic drunkenness a disease, He would have given us a hint in His written word. I read approximately forty verses in Scripture about drunkenness and found no evidence of a disease concept in any of them. I also read verses about diseases and found no evidence of drunkenness being considered a disease. This should convince believers of the error of considering drunkenness anything but an offense against God.

Galatians 6:1 refers to sin by stating, "brethren, if a man is caught up in a fault." The same verse in another translation says, "if any man is caught up in a trespass." Overtaken or caught up has been referred to by one author as meaning entrapment. This author states that entrapment suggests a fault in which a brother is betrayed unaware. He then felt this made a case for alcoholism not being an intentional wrong. If this is true why does the Bible consider drunkenness a sin? What about the account in Genesis of Eve's claim that she was tricked or entrapped by the serpent? This puts to rest the idea that entrapment is not a wrong that we are responsible for.

Our human nature and inclination toward sin can overcome us to the extent that we become involved with worldly things and find it impossible to do good (a good work done through faith in Christ) without the strength and power of the Holy Spirit. It is often possible to quit abusive drinking using the higher power concept rather than relying upon Jesus. Although to quit abusive drinking is positive, if it is accomplished without a belief and faith in Christ, it is not a true good work. Romans 8:8-9 says, "those who are in the flesh cannot please God." Those things not done in Christ are not good works and cannot please God.

I agree with a Christian alcoholic support group when they say, "teaching the alcoholic/addict to quit the undesirable habit or behavior is not sufficient. Sinful behavior must be replaced with new and righteous behavior." This refers to the idea that to quit drinking alone without other positive changes through Christ, is not enough to qualify as good. An example would be what is called "stinking thinking." This refers to former abusers of alcohol who have the same attitudes when they are in sobriety as they did when they were still drinking. It is also referred to as a dry drunk. The real good lies in new and righteous behavior through faith in Christ. Doing good involves much more than just stopping abusive drinking.

Another verse that involves drunkenness is Proverbs 23:33. It says, "your eyes beheld strange sights and your heart utters disordered thoughts." According to the dictionary, disordered thoughts refer to the mentally unbalanced not functioning in a sane manner. Actually, there is a form of temporary insanity that occurs while one is under the direct influence of alcohol, which may explain much of the verse. The dictionary mentions the term "morally reprehensible" as part of the definition of insanity. This verse probably refers to the actual act of being in the state of drunkenness. When the person becomes sober, their sense of reason returns to them enough for them to be considered competent.

Galatians 5:18 implies that to realize victory over the flesh, a person must put their self under the leadership of the Holy Spirit. In I Corinthians 6:9, a strong statement is made about particular sins. One of these is drunkenness: "know ye not that the unrighteous shall not inherit the Kingdom of God, be not deceived." The scripture then goes on to list various sins, including drunkenness. The phrase "be not deceived" may well reflect the false philosophies of some physiological and psychological theories that currently deceive many, including Christians, into believing the disease theory of alcoholism and other "isms."

8

MEDICAL THEORIES OF ALCOHOLISM

We will consider a report issued by a British colloquium of the world's leading authorities on drugs before delving into some physical medicine theories on alcoholism. This report was issued in the 1970s in order to clear up confusion about addiction as related to claimed physical dependence from using certain drugs. In the report, participants gave up trying to talk about addiction. The author of a book commenting on the report said, "experts throw up their hands when confronted with the wide range of reactions people can have to the same drugs."

Professor Paton of the Department of Pharmacology at Oxford University, summarized the major conclusions reached. First, drug dependence is no longer equated with the classical withdrawal syndrome. In its place, "the central issue of drug dependence has shifted elsewhere and seems to lie in the nature of the primary reward the drug provides." These scientists have begun to look at drug dependence in terms of benefits that habitual users get from a drug. A drug makes a user feel good or it helps them forget their problems and pain. These are all constructive steps toward a more flexible, people-centered definition of addiction.

An article in a news magazine put forth the question, "Is there such a thing as an addictive personality?" A spokesperson for the NIDA (a drug abuse institute) surprisingly stated, "anyone with a healthy, functioning nervous system is vulnerable." This statement indicates the possibility that he feels genetics are not a factor in abuse. Individuals often choose a bad habit to cope with problems and emotions in their lives.

Researchers are looking, with growing sophistication, at such clues as the specific needs that different substances seem to satisfy. Abusers are likely to describe unhappy childhoods, embattled family lives and bad marriages. This information comes from a news magazine and clearly shows a stress factor in drug abuse.

A proponent of another theory, labeled "provocative," concludes that drug use is a subtle form of self-medication used to cope with emotional conflicts and shortcomings. This is my view. The proponent of this theory is a psychiatrist at a large New England hospital substance abuse center. Over the years, this psychiatrist began to suspect that the most frequently cited reasons for drug abuse: pleasure seeking and self destruction, are not the driving forces—trying to alleviate problems and emotional pain are. The psychiatrist comments, "I believe if you are more or less in touch with your feelings, if you like yourself, if you have varied and reasonable relationships, you are not apt to find drugs so seductive. A lot of people who are reasonably okay just don't find drugs that fantastic."

A psychopharmacologist who studied for two decades what he called a quest for intoxication of humans, said, "unlike these innate drives; food, sex, and water, the pursuit of intoxication is an acquired drive. We're not born with it." Pharmacologists have replaced the term "physical dependence" with "psychic dependence." Experts have conceived the creation of dependence as an attribute of drugs, whereas in reality it is an attribute of people. Many Vietnam veterans who used street drugs while fighting the war, stopped using drugs without many problems when they came back to the USA. The extremely difficult conditions in

Vietnam were the vital factor in their drug abuse.

Physical medicine theories that try to reinforce the idea of alcoholism as a disease include the fact that upon withdrawal from alcohol consumption, sometimes delirium tremens occur. That they sometimes occur is concluded to mean physical dependence. In addition, it is said that physical craving is synonymous with physical dependence. The dictionary states that DT's are associated with organic brain injury due to alcohol. This does not reinforce the disease theory. There is physical damage to the body and possibly to brain cells from the long term effects of a chemical in the body. These are physical aftereffects from a toxic substance.

In addition to previously mentioned theories that are said to suggest physical dependence in chronic abusive drinking, there are more recent and more powerful appearing concepts of claimed physical dependence. These lie in the more detailed theories of genetics, metabolism, central nervous system neurochemical interactions, TiQ or THiQ substances found in the brain; enzyme variations and neurophysiological variations such as nerve cell membrane transmission, membrane bound neuronal enzymes, and alcohol as a reinforcer.

Numerous research projects and their conclusions make the withdrawal symptoms controversy more complex. We will sort through some conclusions and interpretations of data in more convincing areas of the research. An author of a recent book on alcoholism states that no leading authorities now accept the classic disease concept, yet theories referring to it keep showing up from numerous researchers. A contributor to a book of pharmacy says that cross tolerance between alcohol and other drugs may be due to a more rapid metabolism, since the use of alcohol increases hepatic (liver) microsomal enzyme activity. Cross tolerance is supposed to be a sign of physical dependence. Tolerance is a major factor in the disease theory. This concept states that an alcohol abuser, after time, needs more alcohol to induce the same high that he or she achieved using less earlier in their drinking life.

The author of a book of internal medicine states there are three types of tolerance: metabolic, (the same as dispositional); cellular (same as pharmacodynamic tolerance); and behavioral tolerance. The author states concerning metabolic tolerance that "after repeated exposure to alcohol, the body compensates to tolerate higher ethanol levels." For instance, after one or two weeks of daily drinking, the liver can increase the metabolic rate of ethanol in humans by as much as thirty percent. Another author says that drug dispositional tolerance results from changes in the pharmacokinetic properties of the agent in the organism, such that reduced concentrations are present at the site of drug action. The most common mechanism is an increased rate of metabolism, also called metabolic tolerance. In the case of short acting barbiturates, alcohol, and some nonbarbiturate hypnotics, a more rapid enzymatic degradation (metabolism) of the drug can also be demonstrated in tolerant animals.

Behavioral tolerance infers that organisms can learn to adapt their behavior and can function better than expected when under the influence of alcohol. There are several concepts and theories in relation to cellular tolerance, which is considered a sign of physical dependence, that supposedly explain its so-called major part as the cause of chronic alcohol abuse. One such concept, the theory that an altered central nervous system distributes biogenic amines leading to adaptive cell tolerance, is unproven. This concept also suggests some direct aftereffect physical problems such as a rise in blood pressure during the early stages of intoxication.

A personal observation in relation to the physical theories of tolerance and physical dependence, is that none have been proven to cause actual physical tolerance to alcohol and withdrawal symptoms from the cessation of alcohol consumption. Much research has been done on abusive drinking. A proven concept should have been found. Metabolic and behavioral tolerance are not considered as part of the physical dependence theory.

The coauthors of a book on substance abuse said researchers are frustrated with trying to clarify the mechanisms for the theory of cellular adaptation or tolerance. Reverse tolerance, in my view, appears to show that metabolic tolerance is a probable key to the question of which tolerance concept is really viable in the confusing tolerance debate. The physical dependence adaptive cell tolerance concept would not appear to play a role in reverse tolerance.

The liver can be damaged from excessive chronic alcohol intake. In reverse tolerance, since alcohol is metabolized in the liver and then later liver damage occurs and affects metabolism, the effect would be that the abuser gets "high" early in his or her drinking career. For a consistent abusive drinker, it would take less alcohol to achieve this high later in their drinking career than when they first began drinking. A question arises: how many long term abusers with liver damage actually drink less alcohol than they did before the onset of liver damage?

Because various theories try to explain physical dependence and tolerance as characteristics of abusive drinking, it is possible that something other than central nervous system transmitter-receptor interaction concepts could be involved in the effect of alcohol on the central nervous system. Other concepts make some sense in application to the effect of alcohol on the central nervous system.

Under the heading of nonreceptor-mediated actions of drugs in a book of pharmacy, it is written, "certain drugs may interact specifically with the small molecules or ions that are normally or abnormally found in the body. Additionally, there is a group of agents that act by more physicochemical mechanisms, some of which are poorly understood. The volatile general anesthetic agents (which are supposed to include alcohol) interact with membranes to depress excitability. Their diversity of structure suggests a relatively non-specific biophysical mechanism of action." This concept may be viable for the effects of alcohol on the central nervous system.

In the same book, in an article by another contributor in the aliphatic alcohols field, it is stated, "however, there seems to be little doubt that alcohol, like other general anesthetics, is a primary and continuous depressant of the central nervous system." Since alcohol is in the anesthetic drug class, this explanation of drug action may be feasible as to how alcohol works in the central nervous system.

After studying the physiological genetic theory or the genetic predisposition to alcohol habituation theory, the most reasonable explanation is that some people willfully drink more alcohol than others and ignore even the created unpleasant symptoms. Whether this is due to variances in metabolic enzymes or to a person willfully going beyond unpleasant symptoms and continuing to drink despite the ill effects, it does not involve a genetic theory. It involves how alcohol may be metabolized but not any uncontrollable need to continue drinking.

A study of the drinking habits of Oriental peoples and American Indians suggests that due to a genetic variation of enzymes involved in alcohol metabolism, the ALDH enzyme deficiency in Orientals leads to high acetaldehyde blood levels. These high levels explain the unpleasant symptoms created during drinking. Further, this deficiency helps explain the very low prevalence of alcohol dependence amongst Oriental peoples. Orientals tend to feel sick after drinking just a small amount of alcohol. This conclusion does not explain the tragically high incidence of abusive drinking among the Indian population. This concept only hypothesizes that there may be a variation in metabolic enzymes among races, but not a genetically created need to consume more alcohol. In the end, it always comes down to a simple choice—whether to drink or not to drink. Recently, a physician columnist wrote the following statement in his column: "In fact, the most recent study from Yale University states that alcoholism is not an inherited disease."

A very confusing and complex concept of claimed dependence lies in the disease theory's position that consuming additional alcohol relieves withdrawal symptoms. Laboratory measurements of blood alcohol levels relating to withdrawal symptoms do not show the relationship the theory predicts. According to this theory, withdrawal symptoms should decrease as blood alcohol levels rise. This pattern does not regularly occur. Indeed, blood alcohol levels do not uniformly rise relative to the amount of alcohol consumed. Some drinkers can consume a fifth of whiskey a day and still maintain low blood alcohol levels.

A proposed mechanism involving the central nervous system and claimed dependence on alcohol involves an interaction in the central nervous system between chemotransmitters and neuron receptors, with the natural neurotransmitters. Some hours after

40

the abrupt ending of alcohol intake, the supply of alcohol metabolites is supposed to diminish. A theoretical overload of brain nerve cell activity is supposed to occur when the receptors have no source of alcohol-related transmitters available to them. That is when withdrawal symptoms supposedly occur.

It has been proposed that to eliminate the withdrawal symptoms, more alcohol is required. Even if there is a possibility of some theoretical truth to the concept of the central nervous system transmitter and receptor interaction relating to some degree of desire for the effects of alcohol, it does not explain certain findings. One author states that many studies show that drinkers who do suffer physical symptoms after episodes of heavy drinking will often, of their own volition, refrain from drinking. A large scale study showed that thirty-six percent of diagnosed alcoholics did not have withdrawal symptoms, even when they were still drinking regularly. I can personally relate to refraining from alcohol and when in the midst of a hangover, the furthest thing from my mind was consuming more alcohol. Only later, after the hangover was beginning to wear off did I begin to drink again. Clearly, I was a reasonably long term abuser.

None of this explains how a confirmed and very long term abuser, whom I knew well, managed to stop drinking with no apparent relapse. This individual had been an extreme abuser for decades. Another, who was an abuser of alcohol for his entire adult life, quit drinking in his late seventies when told to quit or die by his physician. Not only did he have no ill effects but he was strong, healthy, and alcohol free several years later.

The author mentioned above further stated, "In no known respect does a person who experiences the physical symptoms associated with physical dependency require, either subjectively or objectively, a drink of alcohol." He also said that the search to show physical tolerance and withdrawal as the decisive cause of chronic heavy drinking has been abandoned by almost all researchers. Further, he says, "As one might expect, the drinkers who have the stronger symptoms generally had been drinking much longer and more heavily than those who had mild symptoms or none at all. The statistical correlations reported in a study may have less to do with the effects of the symptoms than with the simple idea that people who have been drinking heavily for a long time are likely to have more trouble changing their drinking behavior. Habits, associations and life problems would mitigate against the probability of radical change, all quite independent of physical symptoms. Rather than being a cause of heavy drinking, the physical symptoms may be just one more consequence of it." I totally agree, especially with his last statement.

If there is absolute credibility in the central nervous system interaction concept it does not explain the variance in the severity of physical symptoms in abusive drinkers. There is a range of physical symptoms, from the minor discomforts to more severe symptoms like convulsions, hallucinations, and delirium tremens. If this concept was totally accurate, the same symptoms should occur in every abuser after each time they stop drinking for a period of time. The reality is that most abusive drinkers exhibit minor symptoms while fewer exhibit the severe symptoms. These inconsistencies make this concept suspect. If the central nervous system transmitter-receptor concept was totally accurate and if it could cause the more minor withdrawal symptoms, it would still be far from proof of an overwhelming uncontrollable need for the effects of alcohol. The probable cause of the minor symptoms are shown in this book. One researcher noted that a significant change occurs in the level of electrolytes in the body during acute withdrawal. Some of the major symptoms have been associated with changes in levels of magnesium, potassium, and a deficiency of Vitamin B1. Because of this, the proposed central nervous system interaction concepts could hypothetically account for only part of the story, if at all.

Regarding the effects of alcohol on the central nervous system, it is feasible to consider only the actual intoxication except for possible brain cell damage and the electrolyte imbalance. Intoxication is a disruption within the central nervous system caused by morphine-like substances formed in the brain during alcohol metabolism. Two normal physical transmitters individually combine with alcohol metabolites to form these morphine-like substances. Even if these substances formed during alcohol

42

metabolism, they would not account for an abuser's drinking patterns, as some who favor the disease theory profess, but only for some aspects of how an abuser experiences actual alcohol intoxication. Rather than being a sign of physical dependence, the disruption of the central nervous system from alcohol may only be a result of the specific condition of intoxication and in addition to the two factors mentioned above, could be the only factor of real importance that occurs in the brain. How a person experiences intoxication does not enhance any physical need for alcohol. If other effects from alcohol occur within the central nervous system (effects that involve transmitters and receptors) they do not have anything to do with an uncontrollable need for the continuation of alcohol ingestion.

There is a huge difference between wants and desires versus a need or must have situation. A diabetic needs insulin to survive. An alcohol abuser wants or desires more alcohol, but it is not essential to his or her survival.

Something else to consider in regard to the proposed disease concept involves direct experiments with chronic drinkers. In one experiment, researchers concluded that their observations were inconsistent with the inability of an abusive drinker to stop drinking once they had begun. This was found to be true concerning the related concept of craving, in the sense of a person having an uncontrollable urge to consume more and more alcohol during a drinking session. Another experiment left the researchers with the finding that similar results obtained in other experiments disproved the myth that ingestion of alcohol biochemically triggers a desire for additional alcohol consumption by chronic drinkers.

The reality of abusive drinking is that it is a personal choice. No theoretical concept of physical dependence upon alcohol proves a necessary reliance upon or an uncontrollable need to consume alcohol.

9

STRESS

In my unwavering disagreement with the disease concept, I have studied the effects of stress as an alternative concept to consider. I have thought of it as either relating directly to or associated with other physical problems which produce the physical symptoms of abstinence from alcohol.

A major problem in society today is the tendency to look at everything on a subjective level rather than looking for answers at a deeper and more honest objective level. This may be because we are afraid of the truth we will find and fear offending others due to the nature of many problems. It is commendable to try to ease both the physical and mental suffering of others. What has happened is that by too eagerly trying to help in what we perceive as the best way, we tend to communicate the idea of victimization to troubled people, even when they don't deserve that role. Though the truth may offend and be painful to hear, the God-pleasing way to help others is to face the truth and help them come to terms with it.

The field of medicine has fallen into a "victim trap" syndrome by trying to find a medical solution to a moral problem. Medical help may be needed for physical problems which follow alcohol abuse. Medical researchers have experienced frustration in their effort to establish a disease theory for chronic abusive drinking. A well respected Pharmacology book contains some statements in which the problem of determining the causes of compulsive chemical abuse are addressed. One contributor states, "It is quite conceivable that individuals who use short-acting drugs, such as alcohol, to induce euphoria or reduce tensions can perceive an exacerbation of these same tensions (rebound effects) as the drug effects wane." These are exactly my thoughts. Concerning conditioning, one contributor writes, "Drug effects, withdrawal phenomena, and relief of withdrawal symptoms can be conditioned to environmental stimuli." He continued, "The mere taking of an inert pill or the use of a needle or syringe containing no drug can evoke the feelings (including relief of withdrawal symptoms) previously produced when the pill or syringe contained an active substance." This statement could apply to abusive drinking and the relief of withdrawal symptoms. A thought alone can relieve symptoms of withdrawal distress. The abuser who desires to drink during withdrawal symptoms and is aware of the concept that additional alcohol ingestion is believed to help relieve withdrawal distress may be tricked by his or her mind. As in stress relief, the belief actually may be the only factor needed to help relieve withdrawal symptoms. Additional alcohol would only act as a stress reliever.

Another apparently frustrated researcher concluded that "Even a person with a history of drug use and physiological dependence on a drug, might not be an addict. Such a person might be lacking in what we now regard as an indispensable characteristic of a true addict, craving, that is, the powerful desire for the drug independent of the degree to which the drug has insinuated itself into the physiological workings of his body." In effect: mental craving. This researcher is puzzled by people who use opiates, such as heroin, for a long period of time and show no so-called addictive characteristics to the drug. Not all who use opiates for a period sufficient to establish physical "dependence" become addicted. This results in the utter puzzlement and frustration of researchers trying to prove a medical cause for chronic abusive drug and alcohol use.

There are three concepts about how alcohol may affect the central nervous system which appear impressive, but they are only theories. The basic concept was touched on earlier, when theoretical overload was discussed. One concept involves an outside drug taking over and plugging into nerve cell receptors normally utilized by our natural pain and stress relieving transmitter system. The second concept is somewhat similar except that the outside drug is supposed to block the intake of the normal transmitter and in effect, cause a continuous stimulation of nerve cells. The third concept involves an enzyme induction theory that postulates that drugs which supposedly cause dependence will inhibit an enzyme that synthesizes a product important for cell activity—a neurotransmitter. Neurotransmitters sense if an outside drug is withdrawn. The result is excess synthesis of transmitters which supposedly produces rebound effects until the enzyme activity falls to a steady level. This is referred to as tolerance.

The first concept follows the pattern mentioned earlier, which infers that after the supply of alcohol metabolites dissipate then the receptors could go into an overload situation and supposedly withdrawal symptoms then occur. The second concept theorizes that the cells run dry of the natural transmitter and need extra stimulation from an outside drug again to affect production of natural transmitters to satisfy the need.

The third concept postulates the following theory for the effects of alcohol on the central nervous system: Since the initial drug effect is thought to be a result of the decrease in transmitter concentration and then this decrease is supposed to lead to increased synthesis of the enzyme and new steady-state level that restores transmitter concentration, then would it not be feasible to consider that the human body is trying to act naturally in restoring the transmitter concentration back to a more normal level? The above enzyme action is supposed to occur during the actual drinking episodes.

The enzyme induction theory has not been shown to be

applicable to alcohol and is now thought to be relevant only to opioids. This remains an unproven alcohol abuse theory. Since the concepts of cross dependence and cross tolerance between alcohol and opioids is said not to occur, the enzyme induction theory would seem not to apply to alcohol in any proven capacity. The cross dependent concept is postulated to be the ability of one drug to suppress physical withdrawal symptoms supposedly produced by another drug, and to theoretically maintain the so-called physical dependent state.

I would like to advance a hypothesis of one of the more theoretically convincing concepts and will explain a scenario using stress as the major factor. In this scenario, stress would be the vital factor signaling for relief from the neurotransmitter system. (Whether natural or artificial, as from an outside drug that would respond to the call for relief.) If the outside drug is used up, an abuser may feel additional stress along with the partially unrelieved stress already present. This may then account for withdrawal symptoms, with stress being the trigger for these symptoms. There is also the possibility of the direct harmful effects of chronic alcohol intake creating physical changes that are damaging as well as nutritional deficiency, which is an element of withdrawal symptoms. Since the nerve cell receptors are supposedly stimulated by stress and keep signaling for relief, then the abuser's alternative for stopping this stimulation is to try to eliminate the severe stress to the greatest degree possible. Rid oneself of as much stress as possible and, theoretically, the nerve cell receptors won't be as pressured to call for relief. In order for the abuser to relieve the major portion of his or her stress in this scenario, they would need an intense desire and heart-wrenching determination to quit their destructive habit. There must be a determined willful desire to stop the abuse. This is a simple outline of theoretical central nervous system intervention combined with the major factor of stress involvement in alcohol abuse. A desire and effort to deal with the underlying problems that lead to alcohol abuse is a necessary ingredient to stop the abusive habit.

An additional thought to consider concerns normal physical

transmitters. Disturbances in the central nervous system by an outside, unnecessary drug are believed to occur. Theoretically, after the abuser abruptly stops drug usage, physical withdrawal symptoms develop due to a lack of outside drug transmitters. It would then appear that the natural physical transmitter systems would take over and fill the gap. This gap would be due to the lack of an outside drug, instead of a supposed lack of drug related transmitters causing problems as the disease theory implies. The physical withdrawal symptoms would be caused by direct physical aftereffect problems such as an electrolyte imbalance, stress, etc.

Since there is supposed to be stimulation from central nervous system receptors for transmitters in either case, then why can't the normal transmitters respond even when the outside drug is absent? An abuser does not drink twenty-four hours a day, day in and day out. He or she must sleep. There must be times during this period when the normal transmitters are utilized. Former abusers are undoubtedly receiving an ample supply of transmitters in their central nervous systems.

Regarding the central nervous system neurotransmitter theory in alcohol abuse, the etiological theories of mental disorders roughly parallel the basic premise in alcohol abuse. The transmitter/receptor interaction hypothesis in relation to alcohol abuse and mental disorders has not been proven! One author said, "Thus, the hopes present in the 1950's and 1960's for the discovery of a clearly defined, genetically determined inborn errors of metabolism to explain psychiatric (so-labeled) disease have not been realized." An author of a book about the brain writes, "It is naive to think that something as complex as human emotion and behavior could ever be explained on the basis of a variation in the concentration of one or two neurotransmitters."

Since no compelling proof has been put forward by the medical science field relating the central nervous system interaction theory to the etiology of mental disorders, the implication is that much doubt in the central nervous system theory would apply to chronic alcohol abuse also.

Deaths sometimes occur because of delirium tremens and can

be a tragic consequence of chronic alcohol abuse. These deaths may be due to a combination of nutritional deficiency and physical aftereffects, including brain damage and stress. The contention put forth by the central nervous system interaction theory would place an abuser's physical survival as dependent upon the effects of alcohol. We can control our strong urge for the effects of alcohol. If one or more of these biochemical concepts have any merit at all, one can, by determining to stop their destructive habit, control the conceptual stress-related receptors by eliminating much of the stress level itself. This is done by allowing the body to attempt to handle stress through utilizing an outside drug. In this scenario, outside counseling and support helps the abuser. Especially helpful would be calling upon God to intervene in the abuser's behalf.

It appears that abusers who suffer withdrawal symptons, (especially the extreme withdrawal symptoms) are generally not wholeheartedly dedicated and determined to quit their destructive habit. This statement may seem harsh—the truth often offends. It may follow that if severe stress is eliminated, the need for relief can disappear in proportion to the degree of stress eliminated.

Part of the direct physical aftereffects from alcohol abuse could be the suppression of natural receptors and physical damage to some nerve cells. Theoretically, the natural system should rejuvenate itself once the outside drug is depleted, although it may be feasible to consider that the original forced natural system's suppression could require some time to return to normal operation.

The strength of emotional commitment to an outside drug varies according to the degree of stress. Severity of withdrawal symptoms may depend on this variation in stress. Some of the minor withdrawal symptoms, like extreme thirst, undoubtedly are the result of direct physical effects from the drugs.

The disease label placed upon alcoholism should instead be considered a dependence upon stress levels or a people problem, rather than a drug problem. As tolerance is supposedly part of the disease theory, it is surprising to find a contributor to a book on pharmacology stating, (about alcohol, barbiturates and related hypnotics) "With this group of drugs, as with the opioids, tolerance does not directly increase the probability of continued or compulsive use." This statement reflects the idea that even so-called physical tolerance would be a doubtful cause of alcohol abuse. In the same book it was also stated, under the heading of a subchapter entitled *Brain Metabolism* that, "Many attempts have been made to find a metabolic basis for the effects of ethanol on the central nervous system, but these have not had much success." It has also been said that physical dependence is currently viewed not so much as a direct cause of compulsive use but as one of several factors that contribute to its development and to the tendency to relapse after withdrawal.

Theories involving alcoholism are often complex, as well as numerous. Theories about an area like the brain are extremely difficult to prove or disprove, and efforts to do so are frustrating. Fortunately, the written Word of God is clear on the issue of drunkenness. Explanations refuting particular disease claimed scientific hypothesis would not be necessary if many people, including Christians, didn't tend to believe such theories.

Recently, some scientists have admitted there is much to drug dependence they do not understand. Some have concluded that addiction, and even pleasure, are not just the direct effects of chemicals on the brain.

One author felt he could not go with the assumption that drinking is a positive reinforcement because it always relieves tension. He states, "clinical observation has revealed, that for alcoholics, drinking is often *not* followed by relaxation or euphoria, but frequently by depression or anxiety." I personally agree to a great extent with this assessment from my own experience. A psychiatrist says, "the notion of the euphoric, content abuser is false —drug addicts are miserable." I find that later in a drinking bout the tables often do turn and a kind of miserable attitude sets in, although others may have a different perspective on this. I believe abusers perceive that drinking excessively will alleviate the stress they feel. This is a delusion. Since alcohol is an acceptable social drink that is readily available, they put their faith in it rather than alternatives that are often more effective, but more difficult to procure. My original perception of alcohol as a stress reliever, and a very effective one, was such a common belief that it didn't seem important to delve into this area at all. Thinking back to my own experiences and attitudes during drinking bouts, I recognize anxiety, anger, and depression during some heavy drinking episodes. Being anxious during the actual drinking episode may be due to some newly created stress rather than to any lack of effectiveness of alcohol or the natural stress relieving system. In that sense, it is difficult to judge the degree of effectiveness alcohol possesses as a stress reliever. Alcohol is a puzzle insofar as determining how effective it really is for stress relief. I do not see stress being completely relieved due to the effects of alcohol. I do believe it is possible that the overall stress may be the trigger to set off some withdrawal symptoms.

Since an abuser perceives alcohol to be a great stress reliever, it seems reasonable to disregard the theorized central nervous system transmitter-receptor mechanism and take a look at the placebo effect in alcohol abuse. Thus, the central nervous system mechanism is still intact, but alcohol would not be involved in it.

Tests have shown that a placebo given in the place of a real pain pill is often very effective in relieving pain and any accompanying stress. In applying treatment for alcoholism, the placebo effect would mean tricking the natural pain and stress relieving system to help block stress, with alcohol metabolites having minimal effect. In this situation alcohol would be considered a placebo. If an abuser stops drinking, he or she no longer has this perception of stress relief available.

In this same area arises the issue of severe physical pain and related stress. Because severe pain and accompanying stress call for immediate and strong relief, it would follow that a strong response would be forthcoming from our pain relieving system. This may account for the degree of relief received. In other types of stressful occurrences, the timing of needed relief may not be as critical as in the event of severe physical pain.

Stress levels vary in individuals—at times being more severe than others. Stress variation is complex. Both the amount of stress relieved and variation of the degree of stress at different times during the day and during actual drinking episodes, may be explained in several ways. Even with the use of placebos, not all stress is relieved completely because the complex human mind can change directions instantly and often. Changes occur through mental thoughts affecting emotions and subsequent stress levels. There may be stress at any time during drinking bouts also. In a comparison of stress resulting from physical pain to other reasons for stress, the pain itself and accompanying stress will stop once healing takes place. Stress from severe physical pain is generally more intense and immediate than from other causes such as underlying problems involved in abusive drinking.

Other reasons for stress are not so neatly and easily dealt with and underlying problems must be addressed and resolved for relief to occur. These stress variations can account for varied responses of individuals such as withdrawal, the degree of commitment to abusive drinking, the effort to relieve withdrawal symptoms, and whatever else is involved in the alcohol abuse cycle.

Stress is not a biochemical or physical entity but seems to influence central nervous system biological activity. It is a part of everyones life and some stress is normal and healthy. Stress can also be very destructive in situations of physical illness. Stress probably has an impact on many so-called mental disorders. Stress is internal in nature and either a perceived or a real fear can generate it. It is crucial to overcome or at least reduce stress to a manageable level. Some turn to destructive habits while others try to handle stress in positive ways. We must realize that stress is derived from fear, guilt, feelings of hopelessness, and emptiness in our lives. The best advice for people feeling extreme stress is to place their trust in the One who is always there to carry our burdens—our Lord and Savior Jesus Christ. Christ is the greatest stress reliever of all time. He will not let us be tested beyond our ability to handle problems and will show us the way out of difficulties. The Scripture verse, "Let the peace of God rule in your hearts," is for all with heavy burdens to bear.

I am confident that there is enough convincing information to prove that stress is the real culprit in alcohol abuse. A person can allow their mind to dictate to them by letting stress, and alcohol as a coping tool, run their life. Not any physical dependence or tolerance, but the people factor is, in reality, responsible for abusive habits. People *can* control alcohol use. The fallacy of alcohol controlling us is the prevalent thinking of our time. Science is attempting to find a physical solution to a moral problem! It is essential to look at the basic cause of chronic alcohol abuse and not just at the consequences of abuse. Even the theoretical central nervous system changes that are supposedly attributed to alcohol actions in the brain should be considered direct physiological effects of a substance on the body. If it is possible to make a mental decision to stop using alcohol, as many abusers have done, then how can true physical dependency be a reality?

There is much confusion and so many varied theories on alcoholism that we have been left without any reliable conclusion. There is no understandable and absolutely accurate connection between the theorized human body mechanics of abuse, and the effects of alcohol in those conceptual processes. The real nature of drunkenness lies in the wisdom we can find only in the Word of God. As God's law is written into man's hearts and souls, stress arises as a warning of the inner conflict created when we disobey God. We realize within our conscience the difference between moral and immoral choices. It is with their mind that a person decides to make a wrong choice.

Severe stress could be a factor in withdrawal symptoms such as delirium tremens due to the absence of a strongly desired drink. Severe stress affects the body physically and has been responsible for death. One author felt that the chronic withdrawal period is due primarily to the emotional trauma of the patient who can no longer depend upon the seemingly tranquilizing and euphoria producing properties of alcohol. We must understand severe stress and know the possible effects it can have on the body, including withdrawal symptoms such as delirium tremens and convulsions. In addition, stress emanating from guilt, fear, feelings of emptiness, hopelessness, and inadequacy plays a major role in the condition of chronic habitual drunkenness.

Stress has been linked to endocrine and metabolic changes, cardiac problems, leukemia and cancer, weakening of the immune system, blood coagulation time increase, stomach problems, tuberculosis, strokes, diabetes, schizophrenia, convulsions, and only God can know what else. An author on stress commented that all diseases can be due, in part, to stress. One researcher, Mr. Hinkle, stated, "At the present time, the stress explanation is no longer necessary. It is evident that any disease process, and any process within the living organism, might be influenced by the reaction of the individual to his social environment or to other people." He also stated that the relationship or psychological stress from certain physical diseases is less well known and documented than the relationship of stress to mental problems.

Apparently, there is confusion about the influence of stress in the onset and development of physical disease. This may be because stress is an intangible factor, not physical in nature. This makes it very difficult to comprehend the effects of it.

Human beings possess a set of automatically aroused chemical alarm reactions. Two closely related chemical messengers, adrenaline and noradrenaline, in addition to causing visible changes, cause invisible chemical changes in the blood. Stress can increase adrenaline release in the body. As early as 1882, some physicians emphasized that diseases were prevalent chiefly among individuals exposed to and suffering from the strains and stresses of life. Prolonged and excessive stress has been associated with chronic physiologic arousal, which apparently predisposes people to stress pathologies.

There is a strong possibility that severe stress is a vital factor in chronic alcohol abuse, in the beginning of chronic drunkenness, and in withdrawal problems (mentally caused) associated with stopping this destructive habit. A popular news magazine reported that stress was a predisposing factor amongst chronic drug users. This is at least a partial admission by some researchers of the stress factor in abuse.

Those in the medical profession rely upon withdrawal symptoms created by the abrupt cessation of alcohol consumption by a chronic abuser as a strong basis for the disease theory. Acceding that brain cell damage (again, a physical aftereffect of chronic alcohol abuse) and other direct physical aftereffects can occur, the two main symptoms, convulsions and tremors, will be discussed. These are referred to by medical researchers as strong evidences of a pharmacological or physical addiction aspect to alcoholism.

A convulsion is a violent involuntary contraction or series of contractions of the voluntary muscles. Some researchers do not rule out that epileptic-like convulsions may occur even if alcohol is still being consumed by the abuser and after a longer drinking period than what they have researched. Thus, convulsions may occur even when drinking stops.

Epilepsy has been brought into the discussion of alcohol convulsions, since convulsions are part of the epileptic's problem. The term alcoholic epilepsy or epileptiform convulsions has been mentioned as pertaining to withdrawal from alcohol. It has been stated that there are about seventy different causes of epilepsy. For idiopathic epilepsy, for example, no causative factor is known. It is believed that a brain injury or tumor is responsible for what is called symptomatic epilepsy. Tremors precede a typical seizure or convulsive fit. Seizures and convulsions are terms often used interchangeably in similar contexts. Another form of epilepsy is psycho-epilepsy. This refers to a functional neurosis with symptoms closely resembling those of true epilepsy. This so-labeled neurosis is of a mental nature, and since stress is a mental disturbance, it could be one of the factors in convulsive activity.

Medical researchers know that not all chronic abusers who abruptly stop drinking will get convulsions. They cannot explain this satisfactorily and only report that there is a variance factor in chronic abusers. I believe that it makes sense that this variance factor is related to the degree of stress in the abuser, plus physical aftereffects from abusive drinking. These include electrolyte imbalance, nutritional deficiency, and possible brain damage which varies between individual abusers.

A recent article mentioned that what they called "shrinking of the brain" plus early senility were some of the possible effects of long term alcohol abuse. Other effects spoken of were: toxic effect on peripheral nerves, the skeletal muscles, the heart muscle, liver damage, digestive system, and sexual system problems, quality sleep problems, high blood pressure, and a significant increase in the risk of brain hemorrhaging which can cause a stroke. A study at the University of Minnesota revealed a linkage between cocaine use and seizures to a shrinking brain and mentioned similar brain shrinkage in chronic alcohol abusers. The researcher said, "It isn't clear if the brain shrinkage is permanent or affects mental or bodily function. Similar observations have been made in alcoholics, in whom the tissue apparently was restored after they stopped drinking. It isn't known if the loss is in the form of brain cells or fluid between cells." This information is interesting because the public is told emphatically that *permanent* brain cell damage occurs in chronic alcohol abusers and that the cells are lost forever. Now we know that brain tissue apparently has been restored after cessation of drinking and whether brain shrinkage affects mental and bodily functions is not clear. Once again this points to previous theories and misinformation about alcohol abuse that are presented as fact by medical researchers.

Researchers Godfrey, Kissen, and Downs have said that the acute withdrawal state, with the epileptic like convulsive symptom, is related to disturbances of unknown etiology in the central nervous system. This disturbance could be severe stress. Anthony Smith's book, *The Mind*, contains this statement: "Neither the nature of the abnormality (epilepsy) nor the nature of the trigger is known." He said that fits or convulsions can follow many of the ordinary vicissitudes of life, such as fright or worry. This is interesting because it allows for a stress factor in triggering a convulsion.

After reviewing the often confusing knowledge and lack of definitive information about epilepsy, especially concerning epileptic convulsions in comparison to alcoholic epilepsy, my contention is that stress can be a factor or trigger in starting convulsive activity. Brain cell damage and other direct physical aftereffects from alcohol abuse may be the original abnormalities, but the trigger is most likely the stress created by the perceived need for the effects of alcohol.

Earlier, it was stated that a researcher observed that a significant change in the level of electrolytes in the body has been seen during acute withdrawal. Some major withdrawal symptoms have been associated with changes in levels of magnesium, potassium, and a deficiency of vitamin B. One author mentioned both hypocapnia and hypomagnesemia as causative mechanisms of withdrawal seizures, although he felt neither had been proven. Hypomagnesemia is a lower than normal level of magnesium in the bloodstream and hypocapnia or hypocarbia is synonymous with hyperventilation. The level of the blood component gas ($P co2$) determines ventilatory status in humans. Respiratory alkalosis occurs because there is a blood pH problem and carbon dioxide is reduced. Common causes of hypocapnia are anxiety, central nervous system disorders, hepatic cirrhosis and coma, and hypoxemia (a blood oxygen problem). Complaints of those suffering hypocapnia include the inability to catch their breath or to get enough air. Hyperventilation syndrome is treated by re-breathing expired carbon dioxide. Hypocalcemia, a low calcium level, also results from abusive drinking.

One author stated, "In general, evidence indicated a correlation between reduced serum magnesium concentrations and the appearance of withdrawal signs and symptoms." He further says that not all patients afflicted with delirium tremens have a low magnesium level nor do all patients who have low magnesium levels get DT's. He felt that the length of time before a blood sample is obtained following cessation of drinking is important in explaining the variances. These variances in abusers are puzzling but can possibly be explained. One researcher says there can be a sudden fall in serum magnesium concentration between fourteen and twenty-four hours after the last alcoholic drink. We do not understand this phenomenon. This researcher puts forth a few questions to ponder: What are the mechanisms involved in the sudden reduction in plasma magnesium following abstinence from alcohol, and are rapid changes or reduction in magnesium caused by shifts in the distribution of magnesium? A partial answer was put forth by another author when he noted that DT's may be precipitated by acute stress in the chronic alcoholic. He apparently referred to stress caused from serious infections, severe trauma and surgical operations in alcoholics who suffered from DT's. I agree that stress is the trigger, but I would include that it is the severe stress resulting from the desire for the perceived effects of alcohol. Technically, stress may be involved in the shifting or redistribution of magnesium and/or electrolyte imbalance within the body and affect the onset of DT's. Variations in stress levels may account for a relatively normal magnesium level in some patients with DT's. The timing of when a blood sample is obtained may be relevant in this respect.

10

Physiological Problems

There may be a combination of abnormal physical aftereffects involved in delirium tremens. A physiological problem such as a severe nutritional deficiency may be missing in an alcoholic with a low magnesium level who does not have DT's. The level of stress may not be great enough to precipitate or trigger DT's in such an individual at the time of taking the blood sample for testing. These differences could explain the variances in who is afflicted with DT's.

One researcher felt that a seizure could result from a derangement in brain cell electrolytes. Another thought that low magnesium levels and an acid base imbalance are associated with hyperexciteability of the central nervous system. This assertion of hyperexciteability, with other direct physical aftereffect factors, plus stress, may account for withdrawal symptoms—particularly those which are more severe. The manifestations in the central nervous system are those suggesting hyperactivity of various cerebral structures. It is not known if this activity is due to abnormal functional stimulation or is a release phenomenon due to the exhaustion or suppression of a governing mechanism. This correlates with the statement involving hyperexciteability.

Concerning central nervous system neurons supposedly deficient in a chemotransmitter and in order to satisfy a receptor, hyperexciteability may, in alcohol abuse, stimulate normal physical transmitters to fill the gap left by the lack of alcohol. If hypersensitivity of central nervous system neurons is responsible for withdrawal symptoms from alcohol and other drugs, such as cocaine, then why are withdrawal symptoms from cocaine not observably present? Cocaine, like alcohol, is thought to affect the central nervous system transmitter-receptor interaction system by inhibiting or blocking the reuptake of catecholamines (transmitters) in nerve cells. If, after abstinence from alcohol, physical symptoms can appear, then why not also from abstinence from cocaine? Tolerance and withdrawal symptoms are why a person is considered to be physically addicted. Cocaine may be more potent in strength than alcohol. This factor would come into play in the occurrence and severity of withdrawal symptoms. Yet, cocaine has no observable physical withdrawal symptoms.

Hyperexciteability of nerve cells may not be responsible for withdrawal symptoms. This is an obvious conclusion from the lack of physical withdrawal symptoms from cocaine. The basic central nervous system mechanism said by researchers to cause the irresistible need for alcohol and other abused drugs, (proven by the abrupt absence of the drug and later physical withdrawal symptoms) should also theoretically have the same effect with cocaine.

Magnesium deficiency has been associated with convulsive activity and is also known to be associated with tremors, twitching, bizarre movements, auditory and visual hallucinations, stupors, and comas. Patients with DT's have a low red blood cell magnesium content. The author who listed the above problems due to magnesium deficiency also mentioned that these problems appear to correlate with chronic alcohol intake and that none are likely to be causally associated with what he called "the disease of alcoholism." These changes include not only changes in body chemistry but significant changes in the electrolyte content of the entire body. These changes in electrolytes are observed in alcohol abusers undergoing acute withdrawal.

The giving of magnesium sulfate intravenously to convulsive patients results in cessation of convulsive activity. This is evidence that a large loss of magnesium in the body is involved in convulsive activity. Magnesium levels in chronic alcoholics can be as low as forty percent below normal.

All of these symptoms may occur during alcohol withdrawal. Withdrawal symptoms are said to begin within twelve hours after the last dose and may persist for up to ten days.

The author of a book on clinical chemistry stated that, "Little is known about the factors regulating magnesium levels in plasma. A reciprocal relation between serum magnesium and serum calcium levels has been observed in some conditions and, in other conditions, between serum magnesium and serum phosphate; however, no details about the mechanism of these relationships are known." Concerning Tetany (syndrome with muscle twitching, cramps, convulsions, and sometimes with attacks of a high-pitched respiratory sound called stridor) this author said, "Treatment with magnesium sulfate resulted in all cases in a rise in the serum magnesium level and a concomitant disappearance of Tetany and convulsions. Decreased serum levels of magnesium have been found in chronic alcoholism and delirium tremens, etcetera." He also mentioned that serum levels can be a poor measure of cellular magnesium deficiency.

Patients with disorders of the central nervous system characterized by severely low phosphate levels may develop seizures after abstinence from alcohol. The clinical picture is similar in some respects to that seen in those who develop DT's. According to a book on pharmacology, the benzodiazepines or anti-anxiety agents, (in addition to several others) have been employed in the treatment of alcohol withdrawal symptoms. One contributor to this book states, "The substitution of an anti-anxiety agent for alcohol in chronic alcoholism is a common practice, but this does not appear significantly to reduce alcohol intake or in any way to be an effective treatment of alcoholism." (Note: Other agents used to treat alcohol withdrawal are undoubtedly not effective treatments either.)

The same book mentions the use of lithium to treat alcohol withdrawal symptoms. Another contributor to the textbook wrote, "The effects of lithium on distribution of sodium, calcium and magnesium and on glucose metabolism have all been suggested." Since magnesium deficiency is associated with convulsions and the effects of lithium may affect the distribution of magnesium, there appears to be at least a theoretical connection. It is possible that other agents utilized to treat convulsions may affect the magnesium shift also.

Delirium tremens, a major withdrawal symptom of alcohol abstinence, has sometimes resulted in the death of the sufferer. In five to fifteen percent of the patients with DT's, death may result from inter-current infection, associated trauma (as in head injury) or circulatory collapse. Chronic abuse of alcohol affects the heart muscle and circulatory collapse seems plausible. Delirium tremens are generally precipitated in the chronic alcoholic by acute infection, especially respiratory infections. A disease theory is not applicable as the causative factor of DT's. In this same book, anxiety and stress were not considered causative factors and should have been included. Also mentioned was treatment of severe tremulousness or DT's with diazepam, a benzodiazepine drug, to induce calmness or sedation. Another part of the treatment is to supply and continuously balance electrolytes and vitamins, especially thiamine. Fluids and glucose are given intravenously as needed.

In *The Encyclopedia of Common Diseases*, it is written that the withdrawal symptom known as DT's has proven curable through nutritional treatment. In 1967, Dr. D. C. Flink conducted a series of experiments with alcoholics and concluded that the alcoholic is prone to develop magnesium deficiency both because of poor diet and because alcohol tends to deplete the tissues of magnesium. When an alcoholic has such a deficiency, his efforts to stop drinking result in the terrible symptoms that are characteristic of both DT's and simple magnesium deficiency. A rise in the level of magnesium can end the symptoms. Dr. J. E. Jones has reported that later studies of patients immediately after withdrawal provide further evidence of significant depletion of magnesium in alcoholics. He concluded that the severity of withdrawal symptoms when alcohol is removed often correlates with lowered magnesium levels in patients.

Another book reports that patients with alcohol withdrawal seizures had significantly lower arterial and cerebral spinal fluid concentrations of magnesium than did individuals who had delirium without antecedent alcohol withdrawal seizures. In one series of tests, seventy-five percent of the patients developed delirium while still drinking. These two statements appear to reflect a state of delirium separate from the involvement of the tremens factor.

In active DT's, the severity of toxicity, the systemic dehydration, electrolyte imbalance including magnesium deficiency, and the state of nutritional deficiency demand immediate medical consideration. To these problems I would add the causative factors of possible bodily infections, brain cell damage and the stress factor of patient agitation and anxiety. Another author mentions electrolyte changes, nitrogen changes, hemoconcentration, marked acid base imbalance, and frequently low blood sugar as results from DT's. These physiological and stress conditions could help explain when DT's happen during the withdrawal period, with severe stress as the trigger or precipitator.

It is important to consider the idea that consumption of additional alcohol should help relieve withdrawal symptoms during a brief abstinence from alcohol. This supposed relief may theoretically be due to reversing or changing the electrolyte balance. Significant changes, such as a sudden reduction in magnesium, in the electrolyte balance are noted during acute withdrawal. One researcher surmised that a shifting in distribution may occur during abstinence and to resume drinking during withdrawal could reverse the change in electrolyte balance from the original reduction that may have occurred during the early stages of withdrawal. This could bring relief or forestall withdrawal symptoms. This hypothesis derives from the unexplained sudden reduction of magnesium during acute withdrawal.

From what we have seen, it appears that physical dependence and tolerance theories are not involved in the major withdrawal symptoms. Clinical and pathological evidence suggest that a nutritional deficiency is the major factor in most neurological disorders associated with chronic abusive drinking. Malnutrition and subsequent vitamin B deficiency can cause Korsakoff's Syndrome, a chronic alcohol abuser's disorder. Potassium deficiency is common in chronic wasting diseases that result from malnutrition. To the extent that red blood cells reflect the intracellular composition, the ionic composition of cells is altered, sodium levels increase, and potassium levels decrease in chronic alcohol abuse. Potassium deficiency in chronic abusers can influence the activity of voluntary muscles and is associated with withdrawal symptoms involving motor or muscle activity.

The writer of the article, *Liver Dysfunction: Alcoholism*, states, "Alcoholics frequently consume thirty to sixty percent of their total caloric intake as ethanol. Poor nutrition is a major contributing factor to alcohol-induced physical disorders. The end product of all these oxidation reactions is acetaldehyde. This results in increased water retention, which in turn causes a ballooning of cells and subsequent necrosis. Acetaldehyde, with or without ethanol, can cause various organ disorders such as liver fibrosis and collagen formation." The role of acetaldehyde formation from ethanol or alcohol appears to be in damaging tissue cells, such as liver cells. This writer also comments, "Fetal Alcohol Syndrome appears to be an ethanol effect that is independent of the presence of acetaldehyde." My opinion is that some factor in alcohol, when taken in a chronic abuse situation, does physically damage brain cells as in the Fetal Syndrome condition. Severe problems such as seizures have occurred in victims of this syndrome.

An author of a book about alcoholism states, "All alcoholics are malnourished to some extent because excessive alcohol intake interferes with the body's ability to absorb and use various nutrients regardless of what the alcoholic may be eating." This infers that whether a chronic alcohol abuser eats well or poorly does not make much difference. The same author writes, "Just by removing alcohol from the body—abstinence alone does not make malnourished cells healthy again." Further, he reports that, "The cells need vitamins, minerals, amino acids, proteins, fats and carbohydrates, and they need them in therapeutic amounts and proportions." He seems to feel that a balanced diet and nutritional supplements will help alcoholics make a rapid and complete recovery.

A cowriter of a textbook on pharmacology has said, "Many of the diseases of chronic alcoholics occur because they may supply one half or more of their daily caloric requirements by drinking alcohol, and frequently continue to do so for many years. As a result, they may neglect to eat other foods that would balance their diet, and vitamin and other dietary deficiencies develop." There seems to be two explanations for the cause of malnutrition in alcohol abusers and one or both may be correct. A good nutritional diet would help an abuser from a health standpoint and the majority of recovered abusers eat well after they stop drinking, although possibly not the most nutritional foods.

The author concerned about malnutrition writes, "Another aspect of malnutrition that is widely misunderstood and overlooked is hypoglycemia, or chronic low blood sugar." He feels this condition is prevalent in both early and late stage alcoholics and is usually caused by diseases or disorders in the liver or endocrine glands. (Note: I am puzzled why an early stage alcoholic would have a disease.)

Continuing, this author writes, "When the blood sugar drops to abnormally low levels the alcoholic experiences symptoms of fatigue, depression, hunger and shakiness. Alcohol is thus an attractive first aid for hypoglycemia, but it is poor therapy because it triggers a series of chemical changes that soon make the blood sugar level drop like a rock once again. As the blood sugar level crashes down, the symptoms of hypoglycemia return as does the desire for alcohol to relieve the symptoms."

One of the writers of a pharmacology book writes concerning hypoglycemia: "When the rate of fall in blood glucose is rapid the early symptoms are those brought on by the compensating secretion of epinephrine; these include sweating, weakness, hunger, tachycardia and inner trembling. When the concentration of glucose falls slowly the symptoms and signs are referable to the brain and include headache, blurred vision, diplopia, mental confusion, incoherent speech, coma and convulsions. If the fall in blood sugar is rapid, profound and persistent, all such symptoms may be present; in only a few patients, the onset is heralded by hunger or nausea. The pattern and the temporal sequence of signs and symptoms are fairly, but by no means absolutely, constant."

A review of a textbook about the pharmacological properties of alcohol (effects of alcohol on the human body) gives the impression that hypoglycemia is not an urgent concern in alcohol abuse. In another section in the same book, the additive hypoglycemic effect of alcohol is mentioned only in conjunction with drug interactions involving alcohol and hypoglycemic agents. Apparently, alcohol does have a hypoglycemic effect on the body, but the writer was not urgently concerned except in the case of a drug interaction situation. The same book mentions a transient hyperglycemic effect that often occurs during the early stages of intoxication. A chapter on withdrawal from alcohol did not specifically mention hypoglycemia.

Because hunger was mentioned as a symptom of hypoglycemia, and not the lack of alcohol in an abuser's system in this book, it is puzzling why the author (who believes hypoglycemia in an abuser creates a desire to relieve the unpleasant symptoms) thinks that an abuser desires additional alcohol. Hunger implies food and one purpose of food is to increase the level of blood sugar in the body. Glucose consumption or the conversion of food substances into glucose in the body is all that is needed to bring up the blood sugar level. Alcohol is not necessary. It is possible that the abuser may have the perception that additional consumption of only alcohol is necessary to relieve the symptoms he or she is experiencing. Actually, one symptomatic aspect of hypoglycemia involves hunger, or the desired increase of glucose in the blood. This does not imply physical dependence upon alcohol, just the desire for something to help relieve symptoms. Some of the symptoms of hypoglycemia are similar to hangover symptoms.

A newspaper article written by a physician about alcoholism and the shakes said, "Pity the poor emergency room physician who receives a patient in alcohol withdrawal. The doctor has to rule out head injury, epilepsy, hypoglycemia, psychiatric disorders

68

and intoxication, all of which can mimic some of the symptoms of alcohol withdrawal." Continuing, the article read, "In the hospital, the alcoholic undergoing withdrawal can expect to be given I.V. glucose, acetaminophen if temperature is elevated, a sedative or tranquilizer if agitation is acute, and a blood alcohol test. Later the doctor may administer thiamine and folic acid, because these are often deficient in chronic drinkers." This same writer and physician mentioned that emergency medicine is also preventive medicine and the goal is to head off potentially fatal DT's.

The writer of this article appears to separate a hypoglycemic diagnosis from one of alcohol withdrawal. Concerning I.V. glucose given to the alcoholic, glucose given I.V. is also given to cardiac patients and often used as a transport solution to which other nutrients are added. It is a piggyback means of intravenous transport of vitamins, etcetera. I personally checked with the emergency room of a regional hospital of more than one hundred beds and asked if I.V. glucose was given routinely to alcohol withdrawal patients and the responder said, "No!" When I asked if the same type of patient was screened for hypoglycemia in the emergency room, again the reply was "no." This shows the confusion about the importance of hypoglycemia in alcohol withdrawal.

A writer in a book of clinical chemistry states, "The clinical symptoms of hypoglycemia are related to the rate of decrease of plasma glucose levels; if levels have dropped rapidly, a person may appear clinically hypoglycemic, with higher glucose levels. If the levels have fallen gradually, the individual may show no symptoms, even with a plasma glucose as low as 30 mg/ 100 ml." This is a seemingly different explanation from the one mentioned before involving a rapid and slower gradual drop in blood sugar levels.

Although some degree of hypoglycemia may be present in many alcohol abusers, the seriousness of it is not clear. In the textbook of pharmacology, the section, *Withdrawal from Alcohol*, did not specifically mention hypoglycemia as a withdrawal symptom. If hypoglycemia was an urgent concern, this textbook would cover it and any connection to a drug interaction situation thoroughly instead of briefly. Since other nonglucose measures are used to treat convulsions in alcohol withdrawal (and apparently this is a general practice) it is unclear as to what extent hypoglycemic involvement is present in withdrawal symptoms. Even if there was a chance of some convulsions in alcohol abusers caused by severe hypoglycemia, this would not be a causative factor or a sign of physical dependence, only a physical aftereffect of abuse. Possible causative factors in convulsions and DT's are unrelated to any disease concept. They can only result from the direct harmful effects of too much alcohol in the body, the physical aftereffects of chronic abusive drinking, nutritional problems, and stress.

The term *delirium* in DT's refers to a mental disturbance marked by illusions, hallucinations, short delusions, cerebral excitement, physical restlessness, and incoherence; having a comparatively short course. Delirium also may occur during a prolonged mental disorder. A tremor is an involuntary trembling or quivering. Delirium tremens is defined as a variety of acute mental disturbances marked by delirium, with trembling and great excitement attended by anxiety, mental distress, sweating, and precordial pain. Stress or mental disturbance can cause involuntary trembling or quivering and whatever else stress can cause in bodily activity. Researchers Isbell and Associates do not maintain that DT's are caused by withdrawal of alcohol.

Besides convulsions and tremors, there are other problems of a physiological and mental nature that can occur when a chronic abuser stops alcohol ingestion abruptly. Some of these problems are pain, anguish, restlessness, involuntary rapid or rhythmical movement of eyeballs, ankle spasms, exaggerated tendon reflexes, involuntary functions overactivity, voluntary muscle overactivity, undereating, insomnia, confusion, nausea, fever, headaches, hallucinations, and possibly other problems.

Physical conditions may have causes not ordinarily thought of. Fever may be an asthenic fever associated with nervous depression. Asthenic refers to loss of strength and energy. This seems to fit the depression which is evident in alcoholics when what is perceived as the most important thing in their life, alcohol, is removed. They feel they have lost what they need to cope.

There is also such a thing as a tension headache. Stress and tension work hand in hand.

Brain disease can be responsible for hallucinations. Auditory hallucinations are said to be psychological in nature and visual hallucinations may have an organic basis. If a chronic alcoholic has brain cell damage and other physical aftereffects due to the absence of the effects of alcohol, DT's with visual hallucinations can result. Severe stress may be the activator of convulsions.

One author has said that alcohol is strongly toxic to both the brain and the stomach. Alcohol and aldehyde cogeners are even more harmful, which explains the high incidence of postintoxication malaise, headache, giddiness, tremor, and nausea. More serious symptoms occur in persistent drinkers, in whom a hangover may actually be an early withdrawal syndrome.

The minor symptoms of a hangover are attributed to various occurrences within the body. One author has mentioned upset stomach, fatigue, headaches, and an awful thirst as the general symptoms acquired after a bout of heavy drinking. Alcohol causes the fluid inside the cells to move outside, creating a cellular dehydration though total body fluid has not changed appreciably. Thirst is very real and great and water cannot quench it.

The same author states that, "Indigestion is the result of irritation to the stomach. Alcohol is a powerful gastric irritant and the lining of the stomach is severely inflamed. Eating becomes uncomfortable. Food makes you nauseous. You would like to vomit from the nausea you feel but you cannot."

This author mentions headaches and possible physiological causes for hangovers. She writes, "And then there is that headache. Yours may be caused by an allergic reaction to cogeners, the products of the fermentation process which took place when the alcohol was made. Some of these cogeners are extremely toxic and it is no wonder you have a headache which aspirin will not seem to alleviate. Some of your headaches may be the result of fatigue you experience because of a low blood sugar level. When you ingest alcohol, your blood sugar increases sharply, but then it drops sharply and that resultant low blood sugar level can cause the kind of headache and fatigue which lasts for many hours." Other symptoms this author mentions

71

include feeling warm, a jittery, burning sensation, and neuritis, plus pain, partial paralysis, difficulty swallowing, tremors, convulsions, hallucinations, and DT's.

Tolerance is another factor in the disease theory concept. This means that an alcoholic needs more alcohol after a time to induce the same high that they achieved with less earlier in their drinking life. Dispositional tolerance indicates that the most common mechanism is an increased rate of metabolism. Alcohol goes directly from the alimentary tract to the bloodstream and then to body tissues. Calories are produced, but not nutrition. There may be an increased metabolism rate in the liver as more and more alcohol is introduced and is then more quickly metabolized, up to a point. This means it takes more alcohol to produce the same high as before. This would not indicate a disease theory for alcoholism.

Medical science says that all living cells, except human red blood cells, contain a nucleus and that this nucleus controls cell metabolism, plus carries the agent of heredity—chromosomes. There is currently research which implies that since there appears to be a difference involving the production of a molecule and a difference in sensitivity to alcohol, between white blood cells of lifelong alcoholics and nondrinkers, that this infers a heredity factor in alcoholism. God would not impose upon a newborn a physical heredity factor by which they have no freedom of choice to control becoming an alcohol abuser and committing the sin of drunkenness.

The director of the National Institute of Alcohol Abuse and Alcoholism said regarding a dopamine receptor gene study: "The newly reported gene may not be specific for alcoholism, but it may have a more general influence on appetite, personality and behavior." I would disagree with the last part of his comment. A researcher on this project stated, "The Good Lord did not make an alcoholic gene, but one that seems to be involved in pleasure-seeking behavior." This pleasure-seeking concept is definitely debatable.

A news magazine article has pointed out that the basic mechanisms of so-labeled addiction and withdrawal remain largely mysterious. A researcher at a leading university said, "What we do know is that there are very diverse substances. The alcohol molecule is very different from the cocaine molecule and the morphine molecule." In the same article under the subtitle, *A Consumer's Guide to Highs and Lows*, the alcohol column does not mention a specific addiction theory in the *how alcohol works* section. Under cocaine, the *how it works* section does list a specific physical addiction theory. This shows the lack of a physical theory applicable to abusive drinking.

The notion of physical habituation is incomplete at best, and so questionable and theoretical that it cannot be relied on as the answer. Whatever the central nervous system mechanism in the brain that is responsible for the nervous system effects of alcohol in the body is, it would not in any way constitute an uncontrollable need for the effects of alcohol in the abusive alcoholic.

In one experiment, it was found that controlled drinking was possible for some alcoholics. This is my contention. A contributing writer for a textbook on pharmacology stated, "Furthermore, the repeated finding that some alcoholics can drink without immediately relapsing to compulsive, socially damaging use has raised questions about the view once generally held that compulsive drug users cannot regain the ability to employ the drug of abuse in moderation." This is not recommended because once an alcoholic is free of the habit, why go back to the temptation that brought so much misery in the past?

After considering the information concerning what causes physical withdrawal symptoms, and whether the theories of physical dependence are responsible for the symptoms in chronic abusive drinking, there are several possibilities for the withdrawal symptom causes. The answer could be in a combination of more than one concept, particularly when it concerns the effects of alcohol on our complex God-given brains. Possibilities for the withdrawal symptom cause or causes are:

1. Very severe stress stimulating central nervous system receptors to call for relief from chemo-transmitters and with withdrawal the transmitters may be in short supply and not able to accommodate all of the receptors.

2. The sudden reduction of magnesium and reductions of other electrolytes, and other direct physical aftereffect problems, plus stress.

3. The nonreceptor-mediated action of drugs in that alcohol may interact with membranes to depress excitability or the possibility that alcohol may act by a poorly understood physiochemical mechanism, .

4. Even hyperexciteability in the central nervous system due to abrupt stoppage of alcohol intake may not cause physical withdrawal symptoms. As in cocaine abuse and after the abrupt cessation of cocaine intake, there are no observable physical withdrawal symptoms. Cocaine, like alcohol, is said to inhibit the reuptake of transmitters in the central nervous system.

5. The physical dependence theory. Even if there is the slightest degree of possibility of truth in the researcher's concept of a central nervous system transmitter-receptor interaction and the subsequent lack of an outside drug supposedly causing physical withdrawal symptoms (which could be one or a combination of varied physical tolerance-transmitter concepts) this concept still would not be a factor which is said to create an overwhelming need for alcohol.

If the last concept has any validity at all, it would not explain why many diagnosed abusive drinkers have quit their habits and have either overcome or not had serious withdrawal symptoms. Whichever is the exacting and true concept about alcohol abuse (*my personal thoughts lean toward the second concept*) one thing is certain. There is no so-called loss of control aspect that makes a person have an irresistible need for alcohol. We all have a choice. We can stop destructive habits, including those of a nonalcohol nature. How a person experiences intoxication does not result in physical dependence or an uncontrollable need for alcohol.

Alcoholism has been compared to diabetes. Diabetics can point to a malfunctioning pancreas, but alcoholics cannot identify a comparably diseased organ in the human body as the cause of their problems. Alcoholism causes diseases and the conditions of these diseases are the aftereffects of abuse such as: liver or brain damage, dehydration, malnutrition, central nervous system damage, and heart disease. Heredity is not plausible either. None of the possibilities we have discussed can show an uncontrollable need in the human body for the presence of alcohol.

11

Environment and Emotional Turmoil

The atmosphere in which we grow to adulthood influences us greatly. Children are impressionable and much learning takes place in the home, especially learning that involves emotions, feelings, self-esteem, and the ability to relate to others. In an alcoholic home, this learning process is different from that of the nonalcoholic home and can vary depending upon the severity of the alcohol abuse.

The field of psychology views everything in humanistic terms. It also characterizes alcoholics as victims of personality disorders and unable to be responsible for their condition. God is left out of their definition of emotional turmoil and they rely upon human feelings. Often, feelings are wrong.

There is a difference between what emotional turmoil means to those in the psychological profession and what it should mean to the Christian. Emotional turmoil is a struggle within a person's mind and heart between righteousness and sin. Psychology tries to ease or erase guilt resulting from a person's actions by declaring the person mentally incapacitated and, because of that, not responsible. Inappropriate behavior and sin are attributed to a medical condition. This has become deceptively effective and an acceptable means of avoiding responsibility for one's actions. Christians need to be aware of this situation.

During an interview for a newspaper article, a former president of a nationally known chemical abuse center said, "Alcohol is not the victim's fault. Alcoholism is a chronic, primary illness, not a symptom of some underlying condition." Further, "Because it is chronic, it can never be cured but must be lived with by practicing abstinence." Unfortunately, these are beliefs put forth to the public today. They must be countered with scriptural truth.

According to the former president's comment, the term "victim" must take on a new meaning. The dictionary defines victim as an innocent person subjected to something he or she was not responsible for. How many "victims" of alcohol abuse are force-fed alcohol? We must face the true nature of alcohol abuse. This is especially true for Christians. The spiritual welfare of abusers should be of vital concern. The comment about alcohol abuse not being a symptom of an underlying condition has been disproved. My personal experience confirms it.

Thoughts and emotions begin in our mind, beyond the physical realm. They go beyond the reaches of science, and cannot be considered a medical sickness. They are not a physical entity such as the brain, a physical organ. Something that isn't physical cannot have a true disease. The term mental illness is a misnomer. When a person with problems of life is referred to as having a mental illness, we rob them of the human dignity of personal responsibility and the divine relationship by which problems can be met. Though a medical problem or brain disease may bring on mental, emotional, and behavioral symptoms, a person should not be classified as mentally ill. He or she is "medically ill" not "mentally ill." Anti-psychotic drugs are often prescribed to treat what is labeled "mental illness." Researchers don't understand the mechanics of these drugs or how they work in the human body.

Counseling does not deal with the physical brain. It deals with aspects of thinking, feeling, and behaving. It is a form of education—not one of healing disease. A counselor is a teacher, not a medical doctor.

The medical profession's theory that a person is predisposed from birth to become an alcoholic from the first drink, is nonsense. The substance crack, is a drug supposedly somewhat similar to alcohol, although it is considered a stimulant and alcohol is considered a depressant. A person can supposedly become addicted to crack in four to six weeks or less. Are we to believe that these crack addicts were predisposed from birth to become addicted? Some researchers view crack as psychologically addictive only. Others see it as physically addictive, adding to the confusion. My personal feelings are that abuse of street drugs may be in the same category as alcohol abuse. Drunkenness could well include the highs received from street drugs. Scripture supports the case of drunkenness being a serious offense against God. The strength or toxicity of street drugs or other chemicals may be greater than that of alcohol and cause a greater high. This could place greater mental stress on the abuser when he or she is in a sobering up state. There does not seem to be evidence proving physical dependence to cocaine. Since crack is a derivative of cocaine, it would follow that crack is also not a so-labeled physical dependence producing drug. A bad habit should not be considered in a true disease category.

After investigating and reflecting upon many theories about the cause of alcoholism, in the beginning and the end of chronic abusive drinking, I concluded that stress is the major culprit in alcohol abuse. The harmful physiological aftereffects of chronic excessive alcohol on the human body are doubtless involved in withdrawal symptoms, along with severe stress. This contradicts the belief that the disease theories of physical dependence, tolerance and genetics are factors in alcohol abuse! It is my firm conviction that there is no necessary and uncontrollable physical need for alcohol by an abuser.

12

TREATMENT

Treatment of the chronic abusive drinker must involve identification of the underlying problems and emotional turmoil which led to the abuse. Counseling must treat the whole person and be a combination of attitudinal, behavioral, emotional, and scriptural help. A true perspective on alcoholism lies in the spiritual realm. Conflicts between flesh and spirit lead some people to seek relief from guilt, shame and emotional pain. They may turn to the path of alcohol habituation. Man knows in his heart, mind, and soul that drunkenness is morally wrong, yet may succumb to this offense against God.

If someone never touched alcohol they could not become an abusive drinker. There is a reason some turn toward a habit of excessive drinking and eventual habituation. If alcohol was not available the potential alcohol abuser might turn to another habituation or dependency situation. Other habits may supposedly relieve tension and guilt temporarily as alcohol is believed to do. Our first act of drunkenness is a sin and offense against God and constant repetition reinforces this offense.

There are periods when the chronic abuser has some sobriety and can exercise freedom of choice in the conflict between flesh and spirit to choose to stop the habit. This may be extremely difficult, but not impossible.

The responsibility to end the habit may be limited if there is severe brain cell damage. Brain cell damage is the result of chronic gastritis and probably inflammation of the intestines that interferes with food absorption and B group vitamins that in turn damages the nerve cells, causing alcoholic neuritis, resulting in injury to brain cells, which may result in some forms of insanity. It is conceivable that brain damage could impair or strongly compromise a severely chronic alcoholic's freedom of choice. There is a question whether this freedom of choice is totally compromised. There may still be some capacity of reason whereby the abuser can decide to get help. Outside help is vital to convince the abuser to stop the habit or get assistance to do so. God works through help-oriented people and we can petition Him on the alcoholic's behalf. When Christians pray and ask God to help abusers stop drinking, God will direct helpful people and other forms of help to convince them to quit. During this process it may be possible to lead the drunkard to receive Christ. It is unfortunate there are chronic abusive drinkers that are not brought to God in prayer by Christians. Prayer is essential for someone with a serious alcohol problem.

Psalm 50:15 says, "Then call upon me in time of distress; I will rescue you, and you shall glorify me." Christians must pray that the habituated person will not only conquer drunkenness, but of utmost importance, will receive Christ as his or her Lord and Savior. We should pray that the unrepentant believer will amend their sinful ways and get right with God.

To stop abusive drinking is a positive step even when it is done for external reasons without God. In this event, Satan may turn this step into a trick to make God appear insignificant or nonexistent and to influence and delude others into thinking God is not important or needed in their lives. Satan is behind all sin and will deceive us any way he can. We may do things that appear to be good works in man's eyes. John 15:1-5 states some startling thoughts about works done apart from God. One verse says, "He who lives in Me and I in him, will produce abundantly, for apart from Me you can do nothing." Works by man, without Christ, are not good works in the sight of God, even when done with the best of intentions. Pride can cause people to do helpful and humanitarian works but if their motives are not to please God, it is not a good work in His sight.

Christians sometimes fail to understand that God accepts us though we are imperfect and fail. Alcoholism is one failing among many. Stopping the sinful habit is not enough. God desires much more of us.

Sometimes a chronic abuser will try to stop drinking by himself and perceives that he cannot. Though his perception is faulty, outside help is important and immediate action should be taken. Support from others is essential. Steps of the helping process should begin at once.

Attitude, motivation, and sincerity are of great importance to God. Only God knows a person's heart and whether there is an intention to commit the repeated sin of drunkenness. An individual has many opportunities to decide to stop drinking before he or she gets to the severe chronic state. However, a chronic drinker may stop regardless of what point they are at because God will help and forgive us at any stage of abusive drinking.

It could be difficult for a clergyman untrained in the alcoholic's attitudes and behaviors to convince a chronic abuser to give up the destructive habit. A Christian counselor well trained in the thinking, attitudes, behaviors, and emotional patterns of alcoholics is the best form of help available. A counselor who is a recovered abuser would have valuable insights from their own experiences.

Anyone who commits offenses against God must accept responsibility for their actions. We all are sinners and alcoholism is a serious but forgivable offense against God. God loves us and delights in forgiving if we admit our guilt and ask for His forgiveness. We must never feel that what is done is unforgivable. God is happy to welcome a repentant sinner back into His good grace.

If stopping the habit of abusive drinking is possible (and it has been accomplished by many) this shows that we are responsible for taking the necessary steps to rid ourselves of destructive habits. There may be varying degrees of responsibility, especially involving the severe abuser. Some need more help than others.

Christians should believe and trust God's written word more than man-developed opinions and philosophies on moral issues like drunkenness. As concerning other moral issues that Holy Scripture addresses, God's word is truth. Many Christian leaders and theologians follow the disease model. One authority on abusive drinking has said that churches should strongly oppose the disease model. This author states that the disease model regards moral and social ills as pathologies of either the individual or the body politic.

Those who at times overindulge in alcohol should beware because constant repetition of drunkenness leads to habituation. Anyone with a serious mental or emotional conflict who is struggling and has difficulty coping should seek help from a qualified Biblical counselor. Those who already abuse alcohol should seek help from a Christian based treatment center with assistance from their pastor. A recovered alcoholic who is a Christian is good to talk with, especially if there is a wait to get into a Christian center. Most churches probably have recovered alcoholics within their membership. Many of them would be willing to help a brother or sister in need. Christian counselors are available and pastors will have suggestions about who to counsel with. The counselor should be a Christian who counsels with scripture as his guide.

There are Christian support groups available in many areas of the country. Some of these may be denominational and some are not. Nondenominational groups include Alcoholics Victorious, Alcoholics for Christ and Overcomer's Outreach. It is important to have a truly Biblically oriented group as a guide.

The most available option is a regular treatment center plus Alcoholics Anonymous. This is regrettable. We must keep in mind that AA and secular treatment centers regard alcoholism as a disease and often expound anti-Christian philosophies. Treatment programs are becoming more individually tailored and are now addressing emotional problems that may have precipitated drug use. The disease model is still prevalent in regular treatment centers.

Spouses and children must not be forgotten when helping the alcohol abuser. They need counsel and support as well. Spouses in particular should attend a Christian support group with the abuser. Families not only need practical insights but also spiritual involvement of Christian groups. If there is no group in an area, one could be started by a church. With patience and perseverance, it would grow. Close relative's attitudes and behaviors are dramatically affected from living with an abuser, and help for them is a vital ingredient in overall family harmony and togetherness.

A new concept in counseling should begin where the Biblical perspective of the causes of so-called psychologically labeled diseases (in reality, problems of life) is respected and used in the counseling process. We need a type of counseling that combines attitudinal, behavioral, and emotional areas with the most important spiritual aspect. There needs to be a combination of understanding of human behavioral and attitudinal patterns with Biblical principles and Christian love.

Biblical instruction would concern itself with God's purpose for our lives and lead the counseled toward attaining God's eternal destiny for them: life with Him. The practical portion would include common sense behaviors and instruction in Christian growth. This special type of counseling could be called Attitudinal, Behavioral, or Emotional Scriptural counseling. A training format could be incorporated in Christian colleges or seminaries to instruct and train counselors. Smaller churches could avail themselves of these trained individuals by having one counselor serve two or more churches within a reasonable distance.

A good prayer that is helpful to recite is similar to what is called the Serenity Prayer, and goes as follows: "God, grant me the serenity to accept the things I cannot change, to have the courage to change the things that should be changed, and the wisdom to know the difference."

In order to have a lifelong abstinence from alcohol habituation or from any other potentially destructive habit, God must be first and foremost in our hearts and minds. If we truly and completely place our faith and trust in Him, we will remain habit free and be with Him in His promised eternal life for us.

Summary

After years of struggle, confusion, and study of alcoholism in both the secular and theological fields, I have come to realize that the only true and reliable answer to the nature of alcohol abuse lies in the Word of God. As a recovered alcoholic, I have experienced the tragedy of turning to a destructive habit as a coping tool, rather than soberly and directly facing my problems of life.

Counseling of habituated Christians is an important area of concern. Biblically based counseling and the power of prayer are the answer to help people break their habits or dependencies. Other counseling offers worldly and often unchristian solutions, attitudes, and life philosophies to the troubled Christian. A wise Christian counselor is the best counselor to seek. He or she should be well versed in Scripture and trained in the attitudes and behaviors of alcoholics and others with problems of life. Recovered abusers can be especially helpful.

Filling a Christian's mind with unchristian ideas and situational ethics from secular counseling therapies is dangerous. It can have a detrimental effect on a Christian's obedience to and trust in God. I have experienced this, having gone through secular alcohol treatment processes including an alcohol treatment center, AA support groups, Al-Anon support group, Adult Children of Alcoholic's therapy group, and ACA support group. I had good fellowship and support from an AV group and am grateful to AV and the Christian friends I made there.

The mind, under the guidance of the Holy Spirit, is a gateway in keeping God's true faith. When a vulnerable troubled Christian is unscripturally counseled, serious problems can develop in his or her attitudes and obedience to the Lord. Our minds are precious to God and we must not allow tampering with them by unscriptural counseling processes and therapies that are detrimental to the moral principles embodied in the Word of God. Our minds are important in faith, along with our hearts and souls.

Other points to review and keep in mind are:

1. The medical and psychological professions have misled many Christians and even some clergy about the true nature of alcoholism or chronic drunkenness.
2. Alcohol abusers are responsible for their abuse and should take steps, with the help of others, to stop this habit that affects them, their families, and others they meet. It especially affects their relationship with God.
3. Alcoholism is not a disease. It is an offense against God. Many scripture verses attest to this.
4. There is more to a sober life than stopping an abusive habit. AV says it well: "Only Christ can fill the void and satisfy your deepest longing, something no chemical can ever do."
5. If you or someone you know is affected by a harmful habit, seek help from a Christian source that is knowl edgeable about alcoholism. Consider beginning a support group in your church or attending one. If you want to form a group in your church the following format may be helpful:
    1. Begin with prayer.
    2. If you have a Biblical Creed, purpose, and steps, read them, or develop your own.
    3. Recite the serenity prayer.
    4. Ask for suggestions and/or make announcements.
    5. Remain in a group or separate. Have Bible readings and discussions. Let members take part and discuss problems.
    6. If in separate groups, join together after about an hour.
    7. Special prayer requests.
    8. Close with prayer.

Christian literature about alcoholism is helpful and can be made available to members. Donations can cover expenses such as coffee, literature, etc. Facilitator or leadership responsibility can be shared or changed from meeting to meeting. The best groups are committed to the truth in Holy Scripture and look at Scripture as taking precedence over man's philosophy. A group that follows these guidelines and asks for guidance from God will please Him. A Biblical support group is essential for active alcoholics who desire to stop the habit, and for recovered alcoholics. Unfortunately, Christian treatment centers and support groups are not located in all areas.

Exposing the myth of the disease concept can educate Christians to the truth of Scripture and the true nature of other destructive habits and problems.

Asking forgiveness from God is essential for Christians. Labeling chronic alcohol abuse as an uncontrollable disease erases the personal responsibility of the alcoholic for his condition. In what authentic disease does the victim ask God to forgive him? We must not be misled by the disease theory and must accept responsibility for this transgression against God.

My prayer is that the information in this book will help answer questions and concerns about alcoholism and where to turn for help when it is needed. May God bless.

Bibliography

1. Jellinek, E. M. *The Disease Concept of Alcoholism.* Hillhouse Press: New Jersey.
2. Lenters, William. *The Freedom We Crave.* Wm. B. Eerdman's Publishing.
3. Furnas, J. D. *Demon Rum.*
4. Mosby's Dictionary.
5. New King James version of the Bible.
6. St. Joseph Edition of the Bible.
7. Nave's Topical Bible.
8. *Pictorial Encyclopedia of the Bible.* Zondervan Corp: Grand Rapids, MI. 1975.
9. *Facts and Comparisons.* J. P. Lippincott Co: St. Louis, MO.
10. Alcoholics Victorious literature.
11. Monser's Index and Digest of the Bible.
12. *Psychoheresy.* Bobgans.
13. Random House Dictionary.
14. *Minneapolis Tribune* newspaper.
15. St. Paul, MN newspaper.
16. Encyclopedia Britannica.
17. *Handbook of Lutheran Theology.* Concordia Theological Seminary Press.
18. Herbert, Friedemann. *One in the Gospel.*
19. Luther, Martin. *The Bondage of the Will.* J.I. Packer and O.R. Johnston.
20. Alcoholics Anonymous literature.
21. Dorland's Illustrated Medical Dictionary.
22. The Stein and Day International Medical Encyclopedia.
23. Evans, M. *A Ray of Darkness.*
24. Smith, Anthony. *The Mind.* Viking Press: New York.
25. Mosby's Medical and Nursing Dictionary.
26. Knott, David H. *Medical Management of the Alcohol Withdrawal Syndrome.* Psycholmatics, 1970.

27. Goodman and Gilman, "The Pharmacological Basis of Therapeutics".

28. *Stress and Survival*. The C. V. Mosby Co. Editor Charles A. Garfield.

29. Fingarette, Herbert. *Heavy Drinking: The Myth of Alcoholism as a Disease.*

30. *Christianity Today* magazine.

31. Peele, Stanton with Brodsky, Archie. *Love and Addiction.*

32. Meltzer, Herbert. *The Chemistry of Human Behavior.*

33. *Harrison's Principles of Internal Medicine.* McGraw-Hill Book Co. 11th Edition.

34. Davis, Joel. *Endorphins.*

35. Bennett, Vourakis and Woolf. *Substance Abuse.*

36. Harper, Harold A. *Review of Physiological Chemistry.*

37. *The Alcoholism Digest.* Annual, Volume 3. 1974-75.

38. *The Brain.* The Diagram Group.

39. *Alcoholism as a Disease.* World Health, 1973.

40. Petrakis, Dr. Peter. *Alcoholism, An Inherited Disease.* NIAAA.

41. Mendelson and Mello. *Methadone.*

42. Himwich, Harold. *Alcoholism.*

43. *Alcohol and Nutrition.* NIAAA. James D. Beard, contributor.

44. *The Encyclopedia of Common Diseases.* by the staff of Prevention Magazine.

45. Mosby's Medical and Nursing Dictionary. 2nd Edition. The C. V. Mosby Co. 1986.

46. Formula of Concord. Epitome, article II.

47. The Interpreter's Bible.

48. *Newsweek* magazine. Feb. 20, 1989.

49. Bauer, John D., M.D. *Clinical Laboratory Methods.* 9th Edition. C. V. Mosby Co. 1982.

50. Schnegelbarger, Mary Lou. Article 036, AMT Journal.

51. *Fundamentals of Clinical Chemistry.* Edited by N. W. Teitz PhD. W. H. Saunders Co. 1976.

52. Milam, Dr. James R. and Katherine Ketchum. *Under the Influence.* Madrona Publishers, Inc: Seattle, WA.

53. *St. Cloud Times* newspaper. St. Cloud, MN.
54. Hovelsrud, Joyce. *It Ain't No Disease!*. Ark Publications: Minneapolis, MN.
55. *Christianity Today* magazine. July 22, 1991.
56. Waterloo (IA) Courier newspaper.